Rule Your Mind!

HOW TO STYLE YOUR MIND TO LIVE
THE LIFE YOU DESIRE INTENTIONALLY

TEWA ONASANYA

Unless otherwise indicated, all scripture quotations are taken from the King James Version of the Holy Bible.

Scripture Quotations marked KJV are from the King James Version Copyright © 1988 – 2006, by Biblesoft, Inc.

Rule your mind
How to Style your mind to live the life you desire intentionally.

Copyright©2018 by Tewa Onasanya

All rights reserved. No part of this publication may be reproduced, stored in a retrieval system in any form or by any means electronic, mechanical, photocopying, recording or otherwise without prior permission.

Paperback
ISBN 978-1-9164773-0-8

Connect with Tewa

@tewaonasanya
www.tewaonasanya.com

Dedication

To God, the Master Creator

To my family, without whom I would never be who I am today.

To you, who believe you deserve the right to be happy and live the life you desire now. I hope this book brings you love, joy and happiness.

Contents

FORWARD 8
Introduction 13
How To Use This Book 24
The Live Intentionally Personal Contract 27
SETBACKS MOTIVATE YOU FOR A COMEBACK. 32
BE COMMITTED TO YOUR DREAMS. 39
BE BOLD ENOUGH TO DO ANYTHING YOU DESIRE. 47
ANYTHING IS POSSIBLE, EVERYTHING IS ACHIEVABLE. 53
IF YOU GET A NO TO YOUR REQUEST, DON'T BE DISCOURAGED. 59
WHAT'S YOUR PASSION? FIND IT, WORK AT IT, FOCUS ON IT! 63
ANY SITUATION CAN BE TURNED AROUND WITH THE RIGHT MINDSET. ... 70
TO LIVE UP TO YOUR FULL POTENTIAL, BUILD AN IMAGE OF HOW YOU WANT TO LIVE IN YOUR MIND (SEE IT IN YOUR MINDS EYE), THEN ACT LIKE THAT VERSION OF YOU. 76
GO AT YOUR OWN PACE; IF YOU CAN GO FAST, GO FAST. 84
YOU ARE GOING TO THINK, DREAM, VISUALISE, IMAGINE, BELIEVE ANYWAY, ... 90
FAITH AND FEAR REQUIRE THE SAME ENERGY AND REQUIRE YOU TO BELIEVE IN THE UNSEEN. 98
EVERY WORD YOU SPEAK CONFIRMS WHAT YOU BELIEVE. 106
EVERYTHING YOU ARE LOOKING FOR EXISTS WITHIN YOU! 113
FOCUS IS KEY 117
FEAR IS A SUCCESS KILLER. DON'T GIVE IN TO FEAR – IN FACT, DO IT SCARED. 124
YOU ONLY SEE WHAT YOUR MIND IS ABLE TO COMPREHEND. 131
WE HAVE THE POWER TO SHIFT OUR REALITY TO WHAT WE WANT BECAUSE WE HAVE THE ABILITY TO CHOOSE HOW WE LOOK AT THINGS. 138
YOU ARE GOOD ENOUGH. 143
GRATITUDE, VISUALISATION, FAITH, AND THE FEELING OF HAVING IT ALREADY, ARE REQUIRED TO TURN THINGS AROUND FOR YOUR GOOD. 150
STOP LIVING OUT YOUR FEARS; 155
YOU ARE WHERE YOU ARE NOW AS A RESULT OF YOUR THOUGHTS AND THE WORDS YOU SPEAK. 162

YOU WILL BECOME UNSTOPPABLE WHEN YOU HOLD ON TO BELIEFS THAT SUPPORT YOU AND LIFT YOUR SPIRIT. 167
BELIEVING IS SEEING. 173
THE SECRET TO HAVING IT ALL IS BELIEVING YOU ALREADY DO, BY ACTING AND SPEAKING LIKE THE TRUE WINNER YOU ARE! 178
STOP LOOKING BACK. 185
WHEN YOU FOCUS ON SOMETHING WITH POSITIVE ENERGY, ... 189
YOU ARE CALLING IT INTO EXISTENCE. 189
LOOK IN THE MIRROR, THAT'S YOUR COMPETITION. 195
DEVELOP YOUR WILL POWER. 200
MAKE YOURSELF A PRIORITY. 207
WHATEVER YOU ARE THINKING OF NOW WITH FAITH (EXCITEMENT) OR FEAR (WORRY) IS CREATING YOUR FUTURE. 211
STOP PROCRASTINATING. 218
IF IT'S IN YOUR HEART TO DO IT, GO FOR IT! 218
DON'T GIVE IN TO FEAR-INDUCED EXCUSES! 218
FEED YOUR FAITH BY BELIEVING EVERYTHING THAT IS HAPPENING TO YOU IS FOR YOUR OWN GOOD, TO GROW YOU! 223
DON'T STAY QUIET. 230
DON'T WAIT FOR ANYONE TO ENCOURAGE YOU. 235
LIFE WILL GO ACCORDING TO HOW YOU ARE FEELING. 242
THE PRACTICE OF INTENTIONAL AND DELIBERATE THINKING IS ALL THAT STANDS BETWEEN YOU AND EVERYTHING! 246
YOU HAVE TO LEARN TO PUSH YOURSELF, ... 253
SO AS TO BECOME STRONGER AND BETTER. 253
YOU HAVE TO BE MENTALLY PREPARED FOR YOUR SUCCESS 258
SO WHEN THE OPPORTUNITIES COME, YOU WILL RECOGNISE AND SEIZE THEM! 258
START BEING POSITIVE ABOUT WHAT CAN GO RIGHT! 264
LISTEN VERY ATTENTIVELY TO YOUR IMAGINATION, DREAMS, IDEAS AND FEELINGS; THEY HOLD THE KEY TO YOUR DESTINY (YOUR LIFE PURPOSE)! 268
GIVE IT TIME, WORK AT IT, DON'T WORRY ABOUT IT – IT'S ALL COMING TOGETHER. 274
FINAL THOUGHTS 279
40 WAYS TO STYLING 284
YOUR MIND 284
ABOUT THE AUTHOR 332
AVAILABLE FROM DECEMBER, 2019 334

FORWARD

HUMAN BEINGS ARE LIKE COMPUTERS; WE ARE BUILT WITH A HARDWARE (OUR EXTERNAL BEING) AND A SOFTWARE, THAT RUNS ON A PROGRAM (OUR MIND). THE SOFTWARE AND PROGRAM DETERMINE THE PRODUCTIVITY AND PERFORMANCE OF THE HARDWARE.

"If you correct your mind, the rest of your life will fall into place."
– Lao Tzu

"I believe that nothing is impossible and anything is possible if you believe, create the right mindset, plan and you commit time towards taking the right action in line with your desire."
-The Catalyst

A couple, John and Jane Fiditi had been trying to have children for over 18 years.

They had done *all* the fertility tests; and *all* the test results had come back saying the same thing – there was *nothing* medically wrong with them! They had *everything* it took to make babies, but all their efforts seem to end in futility every month.

So they turned to fertility drugs – Jane pumped herself with all sorts to the extent that she was like a dog always on heat. Even the fertility drugs also ended in zero child outcomes.
The more mechanical sex they had each month, hoping in hope, the more frustrated they became.
So they had worked *all* ends with medication, gynaecologists and fertility experts trying IVF once every year for the last 7 years.

They didn't just end there. They also worked with spiritualists – Prophets, Imams, Herbalists, and even witch-doctors. John came from a polygamous home where his father had married six wives, and practiced *everything,* so from a young age he had been exposed to various spiritual *options.*

In a bid to proffer solutions to their childlessness, different prophets, priests and seers also shared various kinds of accusatory revelations about John and Jane's family members, friends and even colleagues, thereby aggravating and complicating an already difficult matter.

At that time they were not aware of how consumed they had become with the *baby thing*, and how deep a rabbit hole they had dug for themselves and lived in. After spending a fortune and wasting resources both in time, money and destroying several great relationships, one fateful day, a ray of hope and mercy flashed upon them.

At this point they had come to their wits end, and on days like these, they sought comfort in eating at a particular famous restaurant where they met an incredibly good-looking, calm, gentle-speaking, kind, white-bearded gentleman.

For some unexplainable reason they were both drawn to him, and they ended up eating with him on his table, and after over 45 minutes of chit chat, they realized he was a life coach and psychotherapist.

According to their report, he was knowledgeable, wise, easy to talk to, and they effortlessly opened up to him about their eighteen-year travail. He just sat back and patiently listened, and listened, and listened as the husband and wife duo took turns to narrate their pain.
John suddenly realised that the life coach was focused more on Jane because she was unusually very emotional on that day. He spoke some deep truths to them that night and as they wrapped up a great evening, they scheduled to see him the following day at his office for follow up sessions.

Several weeks after they started their sessions, the life coach told John that Jane transmitted very intense masculine vibes, and as a trained energy psychologist and therapist, he had picked up the signals. He said that there was an unusual masculine aura about Jane, which she exuded with such power that all he could sense and feel was a woman clothed and imbued in a man's essence.

It was very abnormal because in physical appearance Jane was a chic, curvy, very attractive and beautiful woman. Everything physical about her should have radiated feminine energy, but she was a paradox. If she looked and dressed like a tomboy then it could have been understandable.
At some point, during their second session, the life coach asked John's permission to talk to his wife alone for a bit, and as they stepped out of the therapy room, the life coach asked Jane to tell him about her ideal man.

Misunderstanding his question and intention, Jane smiled and said that John was everything she ever wanted in a man, so he clarified himself by asking Jane what she really thought was the essence of a man. Her answers revealed the real reason behind her very strong masculine aura.

She said the essence of a man was to "Provide for and fully take care of his family, have a steady income, give security and be *manly* in every sphere."

The truth was that John wasn't that kind of man; he had been in the same job role for the last twenty years, earning a stipend from his father's business that he had eventually inherited, so he couldn't really provide for anyone else except to take care of menial needs. Jane however had been the sole bread winner of the house as well as the one taking ALL the manly responsibilities, and securing their future with several investments. Note though that she wasn't complaining about this.

Unknown to Jane, she had been programmed to think that anyone who did these things she outlined was "THE MAN." And the very things she outlined as a man's role were the very things that she was doing in their marriage and home. HENCE - Psychologically she had taken on and embodied *being* the *husband* and the *man*.

This psychological framework had reprogrammed her biologically, such that although she *looked* like a woman, she couldn't capture that essence biologically. As a '**wombed man**', her womb and supposed female organs couldn't conceive a child. Basically her biology was mirroring her psychology because men can't conceive no matter what they try – men just can't get pregnant!

Her psychology was conflicting and completely neutralizing her biology.

"**As a man thinks in his heart so he is**"- this statement has such deeper meanings and implications beyond what we can ever realize..... "**That which you continually think about, you bring about.**"

So having realised this, most of the life-coach's work and therapy was focused on Jane and he worked her through various belief change and energy balance sessions over a period of six weeks. At the end of each session, they created special feminine / ultimate woman affirmations which she was mandated to declare and meditate upon several times daily, and John was also mandated to speak specific feminine affirmative words to and over Jane daily because: **"Words have the power to recreate, create, sustain and frame our world."**

To help her regain her feminine essence, the life-coach deployed several other coaching and psychotherapy tools. The miracle is that three months after meeting the life-coach, Jane reclaimed her essence as a woman, finally conceived, and the rest as they say, is history...

We are ALL Products of our BELIEFS.

Our mind is our most powerful tool and you MUST BE AWARE of what you do with it, consciously and unconsciously.

You are simply a Manifestation of your Mindset.

This book helps you get a better understanding about mindsets and how you can practically take charge of your mind, to thereby create the future of your dreams.

Enjoy!!!

**The Catalyst,
Lanre Olusola**
Africa's Premier Life, Mind, emotions & Behavioural Change Coach

Introduction

*Where success is concerned, people are not measured by inches,
or pounds or college degrees or family background;
they are measured by the size of their thinking.*
- **David Schwartz**

You have to think anyway, why not think big?
- **Donald Trump**

*Thinking big expands what you can do
and what you are able to do.*
-**Tewa Onasanya**

My Story

In March 2012, nine years as the Editor in Chief of *Exquisite Magazine*, I was still going about having meetings to get sponsors and advertisers for the brand. I was invited for a meeting at a friend's lounge to discuss *Exquisite Magazine* and the ELOY awards.

While waiting for him to finish his earlier appointment, I got talking with a lady who was also on an appointment with him. In the middle of our conversation, she asked me a question:

"Tewa, have you read the book, *The Secret?*"

I didn't even know the book existed.

"What is *The Secret* about?" I asked curiously.
These were the opening lines of a conversation that ignited a lengthy talk about life and dreams, hopes and so much more. I left that encounter with knowledge that there was more to life – knowing there is a secret to living life, the life one desired and I was going to find out what it was!

This is how my journey to self-discovery, being aware of life and realizing the fact that we create our own lives ourselves, began.

Let me take you back a bit.

My life has somewhat been sheltered.

I got almost everything I wanted, but I was groomed by my parents not to be greedy, and to be satisfied with what I had.

Growing up, I was a *go getter* – I always went for whatever I strongly believed in, and I worked hard at everything that I wanted to achieve.

I subconsciously knew what the effects of positive thinking and speaking were, and I subconsciously knew I needed to write out a plan for my life. I subconsciously knew I had to be positive to get what I wanted. I say *subconsciously* because somehow, I knew what was required to fulfill my dreams.

This might also have been because I was and still am a Christian. I had imbibed scriptures from very early on in my life – as a child, my mum had handed unto me a book of Psalms, which I read every day. I always recited scripture to myself: *I am not alone, Jesus is with me.* One of the scriptures I held unto was: *I can do all things through Christ who strengthens me.* With that strong scriptural foundation, I went through life believing I could do anything.

I have always believed in fairy tale endings: I always believed nothing bad could happen to me, I believed no one could steal my things, I believed everyone was an angel in disguise, I just believed in the good and nothing else. I always saw the good in everyone.

All this became more conscious when I read the book *The Secret* by Rhonda Bryne, and I aligned it with the biblical knowledge I had about life.

At a young age, before the discovery of the book, I used my imagination vividly. I wrote novels, read a lot and always wanted to have great experiences, not just imagine them. I believed in the school of thought that instead of complaining about something, do *something about it*. I believed anything was achievable, even before I realised that it was possible to create the life you desired with your thoughts. This belief system led me to starting *Exquisite Magazine* in 2003, at the age of 25; a journey I am still on till today!

An example of my knowing exactly what I wanted in life was after a painful breakup, in 1998.

I had recently discovered that my ex, who I had been seeing for a few years, had been in several other relationships with other women, and I was heartbroken. I prayed to God with a deep conviction and strong desire, and I said *"Lord, the next relationship I get into has to be with the person I marry!"*

And it happened, just like I had said it would.

I also prayed to get married by the time I turned 24, and it happened.

I subconsciously told God what I wanted, powerfully and positively declaring, leaving it to God, without knowing how it would work out or worrying about it.

God as merciful as HE is, said YES to my request, and I did marry the next man I dated, and yes, I got married before I was 24! In fact, I got married in September 2002, and I turned 24 in October 2002.

The funny thing is I didn't realise at the time that my request had been granted, it was only years afterwards that it occurred to me!

The Power of your Mind

You may be wondering – what do these stories have to do with the mindset?

Well, whether I knew it or not, I had a powerful mindset that got me to do and receive anything I strongly believed in.

This mindset empowered me to start *Exquisite Magazine,* a fashion, beauty and lifestyle magazine, even though I had a Pharmacology degree.

This mindset made me know what I wanted in a husband, and got me to sieve through all the *potentials,* and not date anyone I felt I couldn't be married to.

This mindset enabled me to find my husband – a man who shared my vision, supported me then, and still is willing to support me through it all.

Through my life journey so far, this mindset made me believe in myself to a point where I feared nothing, and no matter how difficult a situation was, I always saw the end goal and I worked towards it.

Don't get me wrong – I was human and I still had moments of doubt. I always told myself during such periods that I was allowed that moment, but afterwards, I would dust myself, adjust my imaginary crown and I *would go for it!*

I never let my subconscious bully me into thinking that I couldn't do anything. In fact, most times, I didn't hear the discouraging voice of my subconscious until I had started walking on the apparently *impossible* path, and then I would hear the little voice whisper 'it can't be done'. But I knew that I couldn't let that little voice of discouragement get louder, and I ignored it, and continued to believe in myself, my capabilities, my talent, vision, favour and my God-given right that I am wonderfully and fearfully made, and I can do all things (not some things) through Christ who strengthens me.

At an early stage, I believed I could do anything as long as I believed I could. That mindset influenced my daily thoughts, and how I perceived and reacted to situations.

Mindset – What Is It?

Your mindset is defined by the way you have positioned your mind.

Your mindset is defined how you have let your parents, siblings, friends, and society condition your mind.

Your mindset is also defined by how you see yourself and how you react to things – positively or negatively.

Your mindset determines how you live your life or not live your life; your mindset determines if you are *living a wholesome life, or simply existing.*

Your mindset determines how you speak into your life; and how you let people speak into your life with their advice and opinions.

The dictionary definition of *mindset* is the established set of attitudes held by an individual.

Another definition of *mindset* is a fixed mental attitude or disposition that predetermines a person's response to, and interpretation of situations; an inclination or habit.

Philippians 4:13

www.dictionary.com

The Cambridge dictionary defines *mindset* as a person's way of thinking and their opinion.

With these definitions, you would wonder how possible it is for your mind to bully you, won't you?

How Does Your Mind Bully You?

Imagine a bully at school or your workplace. This person constantly makes you feel less than who you are, is always putting you down, making fun of you, and doing all the things that make you want to crawl up into bed and just cry forever (Ok, maybe forever might be a little too drastic, but this bully doesn't make you feel good).

That's exactly what your mindset has programmed your mind to do – to get you worried, only think of worst case scenarios, to always have a Plan-B, and a fear-induced reasoning.

That's how your mind bullies you. It tricks you into thinking you are not good enough, not qualified enough, not educated enough, not tall enough, short enough, pretty enough – the list is endless!

Shifting Your Mindset Consciously

Over the course of our lives, we have been programmed to tilt towards a certain mindset.

This *programming* could have happened through several means, including something as simple as repeatedly watching the actions of a role model figure – a parent, teacher, sibling, or even your societal peers. This programming could have instilled an acceptable thought pattern into us, and could have happened during our childhood, or sometime in our adulthood.

Over the years, I had been doing a lot of things subconsciously, but after reading The Secret and doing some research into my new findings, I began to shift my mindset to consciously live my life by my design, and live the life I had always wanted to live, without limits or fear. I called this *Intentional Living*.

I started becoming conscious of every single thought I had, and how it made me feel. If a thought was making me feel bad, I found a way to shift my focus to more uplifting thoughts.

I began to read more books that were themed around living life by my own design.

A few years afterwards, I realised I didn't want to keep this knowledge to myself; I couldn't keep this knowledge to myself, even if I tried.

In 2014, I started writing motivational and inspiring quotes, and sharing my interpretation of mindset shifting across social media.

In 2015, I compiled some of my quotes into a book (this book) to create a guide to help people intentionally shift their mindsets for their benefits. I call this mindset styling, because there's no one-size-fits-all; mindset styling is tailored to suit each person, just like how you style your clothes to suit your personal style and body shape.

You decide for yourself what you want to be, you decide what suits your life, and you decided how you want to live it; *you* decide.

You are the architect of your amazing life!

I got to a point where I decided to stop sabotaging myself. I decided enough is enough, I was not letting my mind bully me anymore into believing what was not true for me. I decided I was also going to spread the message to as many people that I could, and I was going to help people style their minds to be better versions of themselves. I decided to spread the message: *If I Can Do It, You Too Can!*

I was determined to help millions of people around the world successfully change and style their mindset and live the life they desire.

Styling Your Mind

To successfully style your mind and shift your mindset, you need to see the good in every single situation – *yes, every single situation!* Trust me, even if the *good* is *tiny*, think of it as massive, and be grateful for that tiny good. Once you do that, your focus shifts positively, and you will attract more situations to be thankful for.

You shift your mind from negative thoughts and feelings to positive ones by what you let dominate your headspace, so don't sabotage yourself; force your mind to always think positive and uplifting thoughts.

Don't let your mind bully you into thinking that it is easier and much better to worry than forcing yourself to be positive, grateful and happy. Your ultimate desire is to be happy anyway, so why not do just that and see the results change?

It is time to tell *the bully* to stop; it's time to show your mind who truly is boss!

Your life as it is, currently, is a reflection of your predominant thoughts.

Yes, it is!

If you are not living the life you desire right now, it is as a result of your past thoughts, fueled by your strong feelings towards them.

I wrote this book to help you live the life you desire.

Living the life you desire tomorrow, depends on the quality of the thoughts you have right now. So re-style your mind to live a great life, intentionally.

You are the architect of your amazing life, live it intentionally!

Just like mastering a skill, *mind styling* needs to be reinforced every day and the more you practice, the better you get at it.
 At the end of it all, I am one of those people that just want everyone to be happy, and live the life they desire!

How To Use This Book

Each chapter of this book focuses on one of my top quotes which I believe will help steer and style your thinking in the positive direction.

Each quote is to get you thinking and realising that you have been bullied by your mind all these years, and you are now ready to take action, to rule your mind and live your life by your design, intentionally.

Once you understand the power of your mind, you will begin to deliberately practice how to tame your mind and control it to suit you.

Many of the quotes I have shared are the very words I have lived by, and still live by. My quotes in this book are my own interpretation and can be modified however you want, to fit your own life.

Additional Resources

I have created additional resources which can be downloaded for free on my website. These additional resources are things you would require as you study through the book, and these resources include the Winning Log, which can be downloaded at www.tewaonasanya.com

The Winning Log can be likened to a gratitude journal which can be used to list everything you have accomplished – from being offered a ride, or someone offering to pay for your drink, to being offered free lunch and receiving unexpected money – anything that you have been blessed with. Keep track, you will realise how blessed you truly are.

My Favourite Quotes

I have inserted some of my favourite quotes from various sources that have inspired me, and continued to inspire me. You can also have a habit of collecting quotes that inspire you.

Using Affirmations

This book also has affirmations running through it, which you could use as a guide for self talk. Affirmations help break patterns of negative thoughts, words and action.

An affirmation is the action/process of affirming something or something being affirmed. An affirmation is a declaration or a statement that is declared to be true.

Affirmations have helped me and still help my thoughts, words and action pattern, till today. I sometimes scream affirmative declarations to myself, so my mind knows I mean business. Affirmations are working for me and I hope it works for YOU.

You can also create your own affirmations. Declare them, believe them, and they will become true for you.

The Live Intentionally Contract

I have inserted a contract for you to sign before you commence reading this book. When you sign this contract, you make a pledge to yourself to commit to living intentionally, and following the activities in this book, to enable you consciously style your mind.

You can get an accountability partner to make this a fool-proof process, and you can take it a step further, and decide to use this book with a partner, a spouse, or a friend, so you can measure each other's successes, and encourage each other to become the best versions of yourselves!

Winning depends on how much we are willing to fight the good fight of faith for the life we desire; we are all born to win!
Cheers to our success!

Tewa Onasanya

The Live Intentionally Personal Contract

I, ... on ....
  (insert your name)   (insert date)

Declare that I must and I will live every area of my life intentionally. I will no longer let my mind bully me by settling for a life that is less than what I know I deserve and desire.

I have lived through enough experiences to know that a better life is possible for me.

This is my time to live intentionally, and design my life according to my desire and faith. I will commit myself to do all the tasks required to re-style my mind as outlined in this book; I will recite my affirmations daily, embody the version of me I see in my mind, and change my thinking and beliefs, to change my life.

I will persist and believe everything I want to achieve is possible.

I will commit to writing my winning log to remind me to be grateful for my present and look forward to my tomorrow with gladness.

I will commit to using the tasks in this book which are going to empower me to be a better version of myself.

I will earnestly seek knowledge to empower me and push me beyond my known limits.

I am the architect of my amazing life. I understand and believe the only way to an amazing life is by being intentional in all my thoughts, action, and words.
I am ready to design the life I desire for myself.
I am ready to rise and own my power to live my life intentionally.

....
Sign.

Tewa's Favourite Qoutes

"As far as your eyes can see and your heart can conceive, that's how much you can command and create."

- Udo Okonjo -

— *#1* —

SETBACKS MOTIVATE YOU FOR A COMEBACK.

SEE CHALLENGES AS A GUIDE AND MOTIVATION TO IMPROVE ON THE GRAND PLAN!

Don't let your mind bully you into thinking that a situation is so bad, you can never recover from it.

Change your thoughts, and give your thinking pattern a paradigm shift – look at situations with a positive mindset, as opposed to a negative one.

Yes, in life, setbacks are inevitable; we must all go through some. God didn't say there won't be any setbacks, but He said He will see us through them. The battle has already been won.

You have to condition your mind to see setbacks as learning curves, and as an opportunity for a great comeback; a comeback to rewrite your plan for the better.

You have to intentionally believe that challenges help you exercise your mind into creatively thinking your way out of difficult situations, by utilising the gifts you posses by God's design.

Pulling off the ELOY without Sponsorship

Since 2009, I have organised the annual *Exquisite Ladies of the Year Awards* (ELOYs) to celebrate, empower, encourage, motivate and inspire other women.

For two years in a roll, we had no sponsors and I just about held on with every fibre of faith I could muster. Weeks before the awards ceremony, I was palpitating, having panic attacks and wondering how I was going to pull off the biggest awards ceremony for women in Nigeria without sponsors; right there is when I started sabotaging myself.

> #IAFFIRMBYTEWA:
> I AM AVAILABLE ONLY FOR THE BEST

Instead of focusing on the great events we'd had in the past and the positives of the situation, I was focused on the fact that we might not be able to pull off another successful edition of ELOYs.

Immediately I realised what I was doing, I found a way to switch my focus by thinking of how blessed I was at that moment, instead. I became thankful for life, the air I breathed, food and anything I could think of, just to lift my spirits.

I switched my focus from worrying about what I didn't have, to visualising having a great, debt-free event, and leaving it all to be handled by God – the God that had given me the vision in the first place.

Almost immediately, my energy shifted from being low and tired to being filled with joy and happiness over the success of a great event.

Things began to shift for the better. I was invited by the management of the venue where we had planned to host the ELOYs for that year to discuss ways we could reduce our costs; I also found less expensive and creative ways to get some other things done, and the ELOYs held successfully, to God's glory!

The evening was so inspiring, we couldn't have asked for a better night. No one knew it took a miracle and a half to pull it off, but with our minds in the right mode, we did!

The great event we had could only have happened because we believed our prayers had been answered. We shifted our focus to what we wanted, refused to settle for anything less, and we just kept working on all the ideas we had coming in.

It is interesting to note that the ideas started coming in the moment we saw the situation for what it was – a challenge; and with every challenge, there is a solution and an opportunity to grow. I saw the challenges we were facing as a way to revisit our original plan and make it a better one that would achieve the result we desired. I chose not to accept defeat, and our strong belief in the success of the event, inspired us to act accordingly.

See challenges for what they are, learn from them and move onto the next action plan. Train your mind not to dwell on the negative. Self-talk yourself out of any negativity. YOU have to control your mind!

So the question is – why did we not get any sponsors for the ELOYs, for two years in a roll?

After it happened the first time, I should have learned from my previous experience, but instead of thinking of abundance, I sabotaged myself by focusing on 'I don't want the stress of what happened the last time to happen again.'

And of course, if you focus on something not happening again, it will happen as you have focused on it, and with negative feelings too!

This is why mindset styling is not a one-off thing. You have to constantly practice to become good at it. Like exercise, the more

> *AFFIRMATIONS:*
> I ALWAYS GET WHAT I NEED, FLOURISHING IS MY BIRTH-RIGHT

consistent you are, the better you get, and the more results you see.

The following year, I was determined that this would not happen again. It had happened once, twice, but I was not going to let it happen a third time! I focused on having a great event in abundance and guess what? I did.

Like we do every ELOY awards year, we started off early by sending letters out and meeting potential sponsors. This time, our focus was rigid on getting the sponsors we required for the event. Our focus was on hosting a great event, where all our obligations were met and all our guests and sponsors had a great experience. Yes, it did happen!

The lesson here is: focus on what you want, not what you *don't* want.

— #2 —

**BE COMMITTED TO YOUR DREAMS.
DO WHAT IT TAKES, NOT WHAT IS EASIER!**

It is so easy for your mind to trick you into believing that your dream is unattainable, or that it's impossible.

It is so easy for your mind, people who know you, and your subconscious to tell you all the reasons why your dreams, your vision or your ideas won't work. This is so easy because we have been programmed to believe that things are impossible to achieve.

Never Say Never!

I am certain people told the Wright brothers that it was impossible for planes to fly; I am sure people told Zuckerberg that *Facebook* could not amount to anything. People told me to close *Exquisite Magazine* and forget it, and my subconscious got me questioning if it was possible to sustain my vision.

Right smack in the middle of every discouragement are fear-induced excuses which have to be silenced; you just *go out there,* and do what it takes to make your dreams a reality!

You have to be *that* committed to your dreams.

Do what it takes to get your desire from a dream to a reality. Do not just do what's easier – get out of your comfort zone! Your desired result is in your hands.

Being committed means doing the work you think is hard, and doing what you might consider demeaning because of your ego.

> *AFFIRMATIONS:*
> I AM WORTHY OF MY DREAMS AND DESIRES

Being committed means doing ALL that is required, whether it's making a difficult phone call, or seeing someone, or even as little as getting off your luxurious sofa, and out of the comfort of your home to do what you need to do to make your dreams happen.

We have been unknowingly programmed from when we were babies to view any task we don't want to do as difficult. It's time to retrain your mind to see those *difficult* tasks as *necessary* to fulfill your dreams.

The Bully called the Mind

Sometimes your mind bullies you with conversations such as:

What if they say no?

What if I get disrespected?

The list of negative *'what ifs'* are endless.

The truth is – you never know until you try, and why base your decisions on what ifs and uncertainty? I would rather be certain than regret my inaction later on in life and wonder *what could have been.*

In running *Exquisite Magazine* for 15 years, I have come to realise that even though some calls are difficult to make, and there are some tasks that are difficult, someone has got to do it!

Because I am the CEO, I say to myself: no one knows the vision of the company better than I do, and I still have to work through some things. The not so nice calls have to be made, in order for me and the company to get the result we want.

I have trained my mind to make those calls, ask those hard questions, and see the positive in every situation. I literally *go for it,* and I ask the questions; and if I get a *no*, I keep it moving – not to quit, but to try another day.

This can be applied to so many areas of your life as well. Try it!

AFFIRMATIONS:
- I AM AMAZING

Tewa's Favourite Qoutes

"Everything that's coming into your life you are attracting into your life. And it's attracted to you by virtue of the images you are holding in your mind. It's what you are thinking, whatever is going on in your mind, you are attracting to you."

- Bob Proctor -

— *#3* —

BE BOLD ENOUGH TO DO ANYTHING YOU DESIRE.

THE DOORS WILL OPEN TO THOSE WHO ARE BOLD ENOUGH TO KNOCK, SEEK, ASK, BELIEVE AND ACT!

Knocking is an action!

Asking is an action!

Seeking is an action!

Believing is an action!

Stop playing *warm up* with your goals, by not exercising your thoughts, plans and faith with action; you need to get the work-out (action) in motion – you've done enough warm up sessions!

The clock is ticking – you need to work continually on your vision. In fact, a new year can start for you anytime you become AWARE!
Are you bold enough?

Be bold!

You need to be bold to get to your next level. Take what you deserve forcefully!

Taking it forcefully means believing without a doubt that you deserve it.

Taking it forcefully means facing your fears and feeding them instead with large doses of faith.

Fight the good fight of faith with so much faith that the fear fades away.

Taking it forcefully means killing that procrastinating thought and just getting up and doing what needs to be done.

Taking it forcefully means holding on to what God has said about you, and not what other people think. What do you believe about yourself?

The Lord shall command the blessing upon me in all that I set my hand to.

Deuteronomy 28:8

Who knows you better than you? No one but you! Be bold.

You need to do that with all you can. Be bold enough to ask for anything you desire. Your dreams are valid. What's the best that can happen? What's the best case scenario? If you get a no, learn and keep it moving.

Even during the writing process of this book, my subconscious started this conversation with my conscious self:

What if the book is not good enough?
What if people don't like it?

What if the people you plan to invite to be part of this book don't like you enough to want to be a part of it?

What if this or what if that...

I had to shut that voice up by saying:

---

1 Timothy 6:12

I am the best at what I do, I am me, and no one can be Tewa (you can insert your name). When people read about this book, hear about this book, or read it, they will love it and be a part of it! I also remembered the words of Genesis 12:3 - *I am a blessing to all people of the earth*

I had to boldly declare it and said it like I meant business!
Sometimes you have to talk to yourself very sternly, so you intentionally change and shift your focus.

I have always wanted to write a book. I started one in 2013 called T*he Strength of a Woman* but I never finished it. As I approached my 40th birthday, I decided to challenge myself and be bold enough to fight for one of my dreams, which is getting one of my many writings published. This book is a product of that decision.

Fight for Your Dreams!

This chapter focuses on being bold enough to fight for your dreams. Fighting for your dreams doesn't mean competing or fighting against other people.

Fighting for your dreams means fighting the battle in your head and winning in your mind, and having the upper hand to control your thoughts and your mind to bring your dreams into your reality.

Don't be bullied by your mind, your mind will always believe what you tell it, and what you affirm. This means that if you are fearful and exerting negative thoughts such as: 'I can't do it', 'will this succeed?', your mind will trick you into believing that you definitely can't do it.

If on the other hand, you do the opposite and say to yourself: 'I can do it, I will win this!', and you believe it, and you are as joyful as someone who has already achieved it, watch how everything shift to help you attain your goal! You will start getting inspired thoughts of action steps you can take, ideas will begin to flow to you, and by the time you succeed, you will wonder what you were worried about in the first place!

Fight that good fight of faith. I say faith everything and rise (my meaning of FEAR), with the thought that nothing but the best can happen.

Be bold enough to pray about your vision or your dream, be bold enough to ask for what you want, be bold enough to believe that as you have asked, it is on its way to you, and be bold enough to act on your inspired ideas and action them. Be bold enough to put into action your plan.

We are all born to win!

AFFIRMATIONS:
- I CELEBRATE MY INDIVIDUALITY
- I AFFIRM TO SURROUND MYSELF WITH POSITIVE PEOPLE WHO HELP ME AND ENCOURAGE ME TO BE THE BEST VERSION OF ME.

— *#4* —

ANYTHING IS POSSIBLE, EVERYTHING IS ACHIEVABLE. EXPECT GREAT THINGS, TAKE THE BOLD STEP!

Anything Is Possible, Everything Is Achievable.

I have reprogrammed my mind and every day I am blessed to see a new day.

I intentionally bask in the euphoria of being able to see a new day. I intentionally get into a thankful mode, and fill myself with so much joy till I can feel the fact that anything is possible, and everything is achievable.

At the beginning of a new day, I say it to myself: today I expect great things!

When I just started learning how to shift my mindset, I would shout or scream it to myself, so my mind would know I meant business.

I was determined not to let my mind bully me into thinking that each new day was going to be another drag. No way, I refused to stand for that. So every day, I expected great things to happen, and they did!

Every day, I expect the best case scenario; every day, I expect things to go my way.

Fair enough, there are some things that might not go my way, but here is what I do: I take the lessons from my failures, I thank God for the opportunity to learn a new lesson and I simply keep it moving.

I have come to realise and believe that if some things don't go my way, it's for my own good, something better is definitely coming. I then work hard to see the best in the situation and I enjoy that best in that situation. You have to expect great results and you will get great results, but only if you expect it.

Same thing happens if you expect the worst case scenario, that's what you will get. Classic examples are if you are en-route and you're expecting to run into a traffic jam, of course you will get traffic; if you are expecting not to be able to afford something and then proceed to ask for the price with that mindset, of course you won't be able to afford it.

Why not try this? Expect to win, expect everything to go your way. Take the step with the thought that the only possible outcome is positive and success.

Take a step, expecting the last piece of life's puzzle to fit to get the desired result. Just act like this for a day and see what happens. Expect the best and be filled with gratitude and happiness for it in advance.

Every day, expect to win. You have put too much action into it not to… those steps will add up. Expect it.

Today is another great day to make it happen. Keep pushing on and keep it moving. Baby steps are better than no steps. Expect to win.

AFFIRMATIONS:
- I ONLY GIVE ENERGY TO THOUGHTS THAT UPLIFT ME
- I AM GRATEFUL THAT I AM BECOMING THE VERSION OF ME I NEED TO BECOME TO ACHIEVE MY GOALS

Jeremiah 29:11-13

Tewa's Favourite Qoutes

"The world we have created is a product of our thinking, it cannot be changed without changing our thinking."

- Albert Einstein -

— #5 —

IF YOU GET A NO TO YOUR REQUEST, DON'T BE DISCOURAGED.

IT ONLY MEANS YOU ARE PROBABLY ASKING THE WRONG PERSON OR ASKING THE WRONG QUESTION OR YOU DESERVE MUCH BETTER. THERE IS ALWAYS A WAY, YOUR DREAMS ARE VALID!

You cannot afford to accept *no* as a final answer.

If you make a request, and you get a no in response, you are probably asking the wrong person or the wrong question, or an even better deal is on it's way.

It is for this reason you need to be very clear and exact in your mind and on paper about what it is you want to achieve.

Stop listening to counsel from people who don't know your dreams like you do; don't be bullied by your mind that wants to do things that are easier and less tasking.

Why be realistic when you can be positive? There is always a lesson to learn from the *no* sayer.

Don't be discouraged when you get a *no* in response to a request you've made. It just also means that there is a better way to achieve what you want to achieve; you just need to be persistent, consistent and determined enough to rise above the "no" and look for ways to get a "YES"!

The funny thing about determination is that, the person that once said *no* to you, can still say *yes*. Every *no* is laced with opportunities and ideas to arrive at your goal faster.

FOCUS! Be positive and stand up for YOUR dreams, they are valid.

I can't tell you how many *no's* I have gotten, and sometimes still get – it's unbelievable.

With a mind shift, I deal with every *no* I receive with a positive attitude.

I tell myself that the reason I have received a no is because it's either my vision wasn't properly understood or I haven't articulated it well enough for it to be understood. So, I go back to the drawing board, tweak things a bit, and then either go back immediately and make the request or go back at a much later time.

The good thing about receiving a *no* is that it helps you reevaluate your plan. Every time you hear a no, it helps you see the holes that might be in your plan, and it helps you improve it.

Just keep pushing for that yes and I can assure you – it will come!

AFFIRMATIONS:
- I ACHIEVE MY GOALS EASILY
- I AM THE BEST AT BEING ME. THAT'S MY UNIQUE ADVANTAGE

— *#6* —

WHAT'S YOUR PASSION? FIND IT, WORK AT IT, FOCUS ON IT!

DON'T LET THE VOICES OF SELF DOUBT OR THOSE WHO DON'T UNDERSTAND YOUR VISION BE LOUDER THAN YOUR BELIEF!

Don't ever let the voices of those who don't understand your vision or fear-induced excuses stop you!

If people don't understand your vision or get excited for you, don't tell them anything about what you're doing; just put the work into making it happen, and let your resulting success speak for you.

Too many people are listening to the tiny voices in their heads that tell them: *it can't be done or it's never been done*, and hence, they don't succeed.

You need to step up by believing in what you have – believing in your passion, your larger-than-life vision and then focusing on it.

Like I always say, what's the best that can happen?

Fair enough, some people are needed to help you find the holes in your plan, but that's as far as it goes; if it's in your heart to do it, then go for it!

Don't let your mind bully you into thinking because it's never been done, it cannot be done.

Find that passion, and work at it like your life depends on it, because it truly does!

If you love what you do for a living, it would never feel like work to you. You will do it with the utmost passion.

Always visualise and focus on your vision with a positive attitude.

Getting the Exquisite Magazine Vision Running

I remember years ago when I started *Exquisite Magazine*, I didn't know a thing about publishing a magazine, but I knew I wanted to start one; I defined what I wanted – a fashion, beauty and lifestyle magazine that will motivate and inspire people.

I could see this magazine in my head and almost feel this magazine with my fingers.

No one in this world could have told me it wasn't going to work out. I was lucky enough, actually blessed enough, to have been surrounded and still surrounded by people who thought it was a great idea.

So the onus was now on me to believe in myself enough to want to build on this vision or just stay quiet.

You need a high dose of self belief to be able to talk yourself into going for your passion.

Self talk is just as important, if not the most important talk you can have with yourself. The battlefield is in the mind.

Once you have been able to convince yourself you can do it, the world is your oyster.

Begin to *focus* on your focus, with a huge amount of positive energy, thoughts and action. This needs to be done almost every minute, and second of the day, because self-doubt will try to creep in, and using the word try is just being nice. Self-doubt will creep in, unless you stop it intentionally.

You need to be able to take hold of your mind and consciously stir your thoughts in the direction you desire to go.

In the midst of controlling your mind, remember to pray about what you desire, believe your answer is on its way to you, and just put in the inspired action required.

AFFIRMATIONS:
- I WISH GOOD FORTUNE AND HAPPINESS FOR EVERYONE AND MYSELF
- I ALWAYS HAVE WHATEVER I NEED

Tewa's Favourite Qoutes

*"Whatever we think about and
thank about we bring about."*

- Dr John Demartini -

— *#7* —

ANY SITUATION CAN BE TURNED AROUND WITH THE RIGHT MINDSET. DO NOT BE LIMITED BY YOUR MIND. FOCUS!

F ocus is very essential.

My future is so bright, and so is yours!

Any situation, no matter how it presents itself, can be turned around, as soon as you change your mind set about it.

You can either have a mindset of learning from a bad situation or a mindset of feeling depressed and defeated by it. Both mindsets require same amount of energy, so choose right.

Do not be limited by your mind.

In any situation, take it one step at a time; not the whole desired future at a time, but in day-by-day steps or hour-by-hour steps or even minute-by-minute steps, whatever works for you.

You don't have to see the whole staircase before you get to the top. Just keep going and maintain your focus, and you will get there if you believe in your own abilities.

If you think there are no more steps left, then you can stop moving, but what if there are more steps? What if the next step you take is what is needed to propel you to get to the top? You never know, and that is why you must change your mindset about your situation, and keep going anyway.

A quick example of this point is when I travelled with my kids on holiday to South Africa. At the Lagos airport, we were asked for some paper work which included a letter of consent from their father, his passport data page, and the children's birth certificates.

Now I didn't know about this rule (yes, I blame myself for not checking immigration rules) until we arrived at the airport.

The Nigerian authorities were so gracious to let my husband send the documents via whatsapp and then they just scanned it from there and off we went to Johannesburg.

On arriving at Johannesburg, it was a different scenario all together. The immigration official said we were going to be sent back to Lagos that night, as they required to have hard copies of our documents, and not copies that had been sent through whatsapp.

I was filled with shock for a minute, thinking of the ticket fares, hotel reservations and all that would be wasted – my spa day, all the food I was going to miss out on flashed before me. Oh my gosh, this can't happen to me, I thought.

We were taken to the back of the office where people with invalid visas were and I had to have a conversation with myself to calm down and just focus.

I had to channel my energy into believing that we would get someone that would be sympathetic in dealing with us, and yes we did!

After almost an hour and a half, we verified the hotel we would be lodging, the officials spoke to my husband to confirm I wasn't running away with the kids, and we were allowed to email the documents to the immigration officer, who then printed them and granted us entry into South Africa.

That day, I did the most targeted thought-processing I had done in a while. I was talking to myself constantly, and as a result, my conscious mind was louder than my subconscious mind. In the end it paid off.

Any situation can be turned around, if you can shift your focus to what you want, and refuse to sabotage yourself by doing otherwise. You also have to believe that it is possible.

Be focused and optimistic.

Trust me when I say everything will be rearranged (spiritually and miraculously) to make your desire a reality. The only catch is to believe when you ask, and have unwavering faith that you will get what you want.

FOCUS IS KEY!

AFFIRMATIONS:
- I AM VICTORIOUS
- I AM EFFORTLESSLY FLOURISING IN THE LAND

— #8 —

TO LIVE UP TO YOUR FULL POTENTIAL, BUILD AN IMAGE OF HOW YOU WANT TO LIVE IN YOUR MIND (SEE IT IN YOUR MINDS EYE), THEN ACT LIKE THAT VERSION OF YOU.

TO LIVE UP TO YOUR FULL POTENTIAL, BUILD AN IMAGE OF HOW YOU WANT TO LIVE IN YOUR MIND (SEE IT IN YOUR MINDS EYE), THEN ACT LIKE THAT VERSION OF YOU.

Everything is possible for him who believes.

To fulfill your potential, you need to master the art of visualising.

I usually visualize by lighting a scented candle, inhaling its exquisitely captivating fragrance and imagining the best case scenario for anything I desire.

If you can't see yourself achieving what you set out to achieve in your mind, then it can't happen. That's the rule of life.

If you can see it in your head, you can hold it in your hands, by following the inspired action you act on.

See the vision, write it out, say it, and make it plain so your mind knows you mean business. Don't let your mind bully you. You know what you want, hold that vision, and focus on it until it becomes your reality.

My Happy Colour

During a television appearance, I wore a yellow dress. Sometimes, I opt to wear yellow without thinking about it or paying any attention to the effect it has on me.

But on this particular day, I was filled with so much gratitude for life and I chose to be happy and radiant for some reason. That day, almost everyone I came in contact with paid me a compliment.

By the end of that day, I realised I had found my *happy colour;* the colour that embodied who I was and I am - radiant, happy, inspiring, passionate, encouraging, loving and positive!

From that day onwards, I embodied the fact that I desire to radiate light and love wherever I go, and that's what I do till date. I have embodied that light.

Now, I dress the way I feel on the inside.

When I'm feeling bold, I go for a strong look. I don't want to blend in – I want to stand out in the most positive light.

My look tells a story of who I am. I totally embody my evolution into my best self, and I don't let my mind bully me to thinking otherwise.

So, build that image of you in your head, and in your life; slaying your goals, building your dreams and impacting lives whilst at it! Believe me – someone is being inspired by just watching you.

Visualise and feel it, then act like it. Act like the only result possible for the "Queen You" or the "King You" is success and the best case scenario.

TO LIVE UP TO YOUR FULL POTENTIAL, BUILD AN IMAGE OF HOW YOU WANT TO LIVE IN YOUR MIND (SEE IT IN YOUR MINDS EYE), THEN ACT LIKE THAT VERSION OF YOU.

Try visualizing and acting like the success you want to be. Try it and see if it works.

Do not think of the possibility of it not working out.

Instead of thinking "what if when I jump, I fall?" Try to think "what if when I jump, I fly?"

You were born to win; it only depends on how much you want to.

AFFIRMATIONS:
- ABUNDANCE IS MY BIRTHRIGHT
- I ALWAYS PROSPER NO MATTER WHAT

Tewa's Favourite Qoutes

"To accomplish great things, we must first dream, then visualize, then plan, believe act."
"

- Alfred A. Montapert -

— #9 —

**GO AT YOUR OWN PACE; IF YOU CAN GO FAST, GO FAST.
IF YOU CAN GO SLOW, GO SLOW.
RUN YOUR OWN RACE AND KEEP IT MOVING.
BABY STEPS ARE BETTER THAN NO STEPS AT ALL.**

Go At Your Own Pace; If You Can Go Fast, Go Fast.

Whatever your pace, keep it moving in the direction you want to go. You are allowed to change course anytime; it's your life, YOU decide!

Run your own course and stop getting distracted by what other people are doing or what others have achieved that you haven't.

We all have our own set time, which is unique to us. You cannot compare someone else's chapter to yours. No two people in this world are the same, so why would you expect that your life race and experiences will be similar to someone else's?

If your pace is to run as fast as you possibly can, then do that. If your pace is to go slowly and steadily, by all means do that, but remember to keep one thing in mind: you are moving, not just moving, but moving in the direction of your dreams.

Don't let your mind trick you into believing your friends or your siblings, or other people are doing better than you are; don't let your mind worry you into doing the things you are not supposed to be doing. Your life journey is specific to you, so go at your pace.

Stop comparing yourself to others. Be committed to being the best you.

A big joy killer and complete waste of energy is checking other people's life-seasons and comparing yourself to them. Aside from the fact that it is a big insult to you, comparing the unique you to anyone else is highly unnecessary.

Stop checking to see if the grass in someone else's yard is greener than yours – instead, concentrate on watering yours to make it the best it can possibly be.

Believe this, everyone is battling their minds and working to be the best they want to be. Yes, there are people who are constantly comparing themselves to everyone else, but it doesn't serve any good purpose, other than make them feel sad.

Be so invested in yourself that you have no time to think of who is doing better than you are.

If you take a poll, you will soon realise that everyone is work in progress.

I remember a few years ago, I started thinking of all the things I should have accomplished by a certain age, and all the things Exquisite Magazine should have achieved by a certain time or milestone. By the end of that day, I had successfully belittled all my past work and experiences and felt sad.

A conversation with someone who had called me out of the blue shocked me out of my thinking, and made me eventually realise what I was doing.

She called to tell me how she marveled at how I had succeeded in getting to the level where I was, and she went on about how she was impressed by my work and was wondering if I could advise her on how to continue on her own journey!

After that conversation, I realised that over the years, as a person and as a business woman, I had grown in knowledge and understanding, which I am now able to share to inspire other people.

Not being where I thought I should be, should never have been in question. Instead, I should have focused on the fact that I am where I am, and I have survived many battles.

Keeping track and watching what others were doing was not serving my higher purpose, therefore, I had to change my thinking, get my mind in check and appreciate my journey and celebrate where I currently was.

We all have different experiences. Competing or looking at other people's progress just robs you of the joy of appreciating where you are, and the excitement of where you are going.

If you evaluate yourself, you will realise you have been winning.

You are here aren't you? You are reading this aren't you?

You are alive; you are winning!!!

AFFIRMATIONS:
- I AM BLESSED
- I ATTRACT BLESSINGS

— *#10* —

YOU ARE GOING TO THINK, DREAM, VISUALISE, IMAGINE, BELIEVE ANYWAY,

MAKE IT BIG AND POSITIVE ABOUT WHAT YOU WANT. WE ARE ALL BORN TO WIN; YOU DECIDE!

Think it. Say it. Visualise it. Declare it. Work at it, and then Take Over! As a man thinks, so is he.

You are going to think anyway, you might as well make it about things you want. You are going to dream or visualise anyway, it makes sense to only visualise and dream about what you want.

What's the point of doing otherwise? If it's not the result you want, don't waste your thinking energy on it.

The day I figured this out, I was like, *Oh my gosh, this is it! Thank you Lord for the revelation!*

Everything requires the same energy; thinking of a small thing, thinking of a big thing, the bottom line is, if thinking takes the same energy, why not milk it and think big, massive, mega positive thoughts? Mix your thoughts with great feelings of joy, happiness and gratitude!

Do you believe we are all born to win?

I do! I believe we are all equipped with what we require to succeed, it just depends on the amount of work we are willing to do, to discover our true self and run with it.

What is it that you want? What version of yourself do you want to be?

Whatever it is, visualise it and try as much as possible to embody it every single day till you become that version.

Identify habits that do not serve your higher purpose. Identify traits or energy that do not uplift you and do away with them.

Take note that you would need to carefully analyse yourself to know what habits you need to get rid of, and which ones you need to amplify. It might take a while, but get busy getting to know yourself – you won't believe what you will discover.

Drop any habit that does not serve your highest version. You owe it to yourself to walk away from things that hold you back.

I constantly get to know myself, by creating an atmosphere around me that I love. I light a scented candle or burn incense or oil. I play soft music in the background or just listen to a recording of waves flowing at the beach or droplets of water or listen to a recording of my affirmations on repeat; these things relax me.

I immerse myself in that atmosphere and I do a self examination and ask questions such as: What do I like? What do I want? Why do I want this or that? What do I need to do to get this or that result?

I start a conversation with myself and trust me, soon the creative juices start to flow and I get my notebook and begin to write fresh thoughts and ideas that come to me.

Find what suits you and embody it till your mind believes it, and then it becomes your reality.

Proverbs 23:7

Fight the good fight to be positive all the time; dream, visualise and believe that only the best can come to you.

AFFIRMATIONS:
- I ATTRACT POSITIVE PEOPLE
- I WILL DO BETTER FOR MYSELF

Tewa's Favourite Qoutes

"Your whole life is a manifestation of the thoughts that go on in your head."

- Lisa Nichols -

— *#11* —

FAITH AND FEAR REQUIRE THE SAME ENERGY AND REQUIRE YOU TO BELIEVE IN THE UNSEEN.

DO YOURSELF A FAVOUR, AND CHOOSE FAITH!

I have so many favourite quotes, and this is one of them.

I had an amazing *wow* moment the day this was revealed to me.

Fear and FAITH require you to believe in the unseen.

Fear requires you to believe in the unseen, but so does FAITH. Why do we then choose to *fear* instead of *faith the unknown?*

Like I mentioned earlier, the reason is that we have been programmed or wired by the society to always think of the worst case scenario.

When I say *programmed*, I mean our whole life has been built around several well-known and widely accepted *myths* which originate from a place of fear. I will counter some of these *myths* from my version of the place of faith.

MYTH #1: I must work hard to be rich

Instead of saying this, rephrase this and say: I must work *smart* and *strategically* to be rich.

There is no doubt that work has to be done to be rich, but it doesn't have to be doing jobs you hate; you can work passionately hard on something you love, that way it is not a job you hate, but something you love.

The reason they call it *hard work* is because nothing good comes from your comfort zone; it will require you to think outside the box, or think with no box in mind, basically, think, make some decisions and *King or Queen Up!*

Many people want things handed to them, but don't want to do the work required or the difficult tasks, hence it becomes *hard work*. Get it?

MYTH #2: Expect the Worst Case Scenario

Why must we be told to expect the worst case scenario? I don't get this. I really don't.

Why worry about something going wrong (fear) when you can be happy that it will go right (faith)?

Both outcomes require the same energy anyway, and in both circumstances, you believe in something you haven't seen yet.

It's an obvious no-brainer; expect the best case scenario instead! Be happy about the fact that things will go your way, and do not worry about it.

Worrying and expecting the worst case scenario will only rob you of the joy you should feel in the present. Don't be bullied by your mind, choose right!

MYTH #3: I Should Be Afraid of the unknown

Why should I *fear* the unknown when I can have faith in the unknown?

It's the same mind thinking, it's the same feeling, only that one will lift your spirit (faith) and the other will make you unhappy and depressed (fear).

Why should you be fearful of the unknown? Instead, have faith in the unknown! Be happy knowing the unknown will serve your higher purpose and it will be what you have been praying for. Say *yes* to a great unknown, knowing that in that unknown, your dreams are valid and fulfilled!

MYTH #4: Always have a Plan B

Having a Plan B already means you believe that Plan A will fail.

Instead of calling it a Plan B, why not call it a modification to the original plan? Why not look at the original plan A that didn't work as a learning curve to make amends and get it right?

There shouldn't be a Plan B; instead, learn a lesson from Plan A, and modify it to reach your goal.

Stop the fear-induced excuses of having a Plan B which indicates that you believe the unknown reason why Plan A will fail.

I look at things this way: if Plan A doesn't work, then I need to learn a lesson from it and then modify it. Remember, all things work together for good.

MYTH #5: Seeing is Believing

I talk about this statement more in another quote, this statement indicates fear.

Instead, rephrase this to *believing is seeing*, because if you do not believe in something, you can't see it in your mind or your reality.

If you don't believe and have the commitment, you won't be able to drive it.

If I didn't believe I could write this book and more, it would not come to fruition.

You cannot believe everything you see in real life, especially if what you are seeing is not the outcome you want. Believe first, visualise it and then see it in your mind, then it will manifest in your reality.

MYH #6: Nothing Comes Easy

Who ever thought of this pessimistic way of thinking and living life?

I believe life is not that difficult, we make it difficult. Why base your life's work or decisions on the fact that *nothing comes easy?*

I think everything comes easy to those who want it, it just requires work. Just like you can't expect a baby to start talking immediately it's born, that's the way you can't expect to live your dreams now, without learning about what it requires and then grow through the journey.

Of course people will say it's not easy because you have to put in the work, which is usually not in your comfort zone, and it requires you to do tasks which you might not necessarily like.

Did I like waking up at 2am to work on my book and get my head right? No, but it's what I needed to do to get my results.

Do I enjoy doing ab exercises regularly because I want to have a washboard tummy? No I don't, but it has to be done.

Do I enjoy studying regularly so I can pass some exams? No, but it has to be done.

I can go on about the things I have to do to get what I want, they are not so easy to do sometimes, but they are required.

Consistency is of great importance.

AFFIRMATIONS:
- I AM READY TO BE SHOWERED WITH BRAND NEW BLESSINGS
- I AM THE ARCHITECT OF MY AMAZING LIFE

— *#12* —

**EVERY WORD YOU SPEAK CONFIRMS WHAT YOU BELIEVE.
SPEAK ONLY OF WHAT YOU DESIRE!**

> *From the fruit of his mouth a man's stomach is filled with
> the harvest from his lips he is satisfied.*
> Proverbs 18: 20

> *The tongue has the power of life and death
> and those who love it will eat its fruit.*
> Proverbs 18: 21

You need to cultivate that habit of speaking only of what you desire.

I am growing at this too. Yes, we are human and sometimes there are certain points in our lives when things get overwhelming and we feel like giving up. During those moments, we are allowed to *feel down,* but not *remain down,* and wallow in self-pity. There might be moments when you need to let things out, but afterwards, dust yourself off and keep it moving.

The power of the tongue, the power of words; let's not forget the power of thoughts, because our thoughts become the words we speak. Watch what you say. Speak only of what you desire.

Have you ever heard of the word abracadabra? It's a Hebrew word that means *I CREATE WHAT I SPEAK.* I guess that is the reason why magicians say abracadabra before they conjure anything.

I don't know about you, but I just assumed *abracadabra* was gibberish that was made up until I came to the knowledge that *abracadabra* is actually a word in Hebrew language!

If we create what we speak, it is just safe to only talk about what you want to be and nothing else. I work at this every day.

Switch over to victory talk.

Speak only of what you want. If it's not in line with what you want, try your hardest not to talk about it. Don't let your mind bully you into saying what you don't desire.

Saying it, is affirming it to yourself.
I know it can be tough to abide by this rule – I go through it too, after all, we are all human, but you need to keep practicing it till it becomes you.

Fight the good fight for what you want with your conscious and subconscious mind, and you will win. Believe you will, and you will. Speak what you want till it manifests.

AFFIRMATIONS:
- I HAVE UNLIMITED FAITH
- I ACKNOWLEGDE MY POWER AND I WILL USE MY MIND RIGHT

Tewa's Favourite Qoutes

"When you focus on something, no matter what it happens to be, you are calling that into existence."

– Lisa Nichols –

— *#13* —

EVERYTHING YOU ARE LOOKING FOR EXISTS WITHIN YOU!

To succeed in life, you have to dig deep within yourself – it's an inside job.

You are more powerful than you know.

Look deep within you and connect with yourself in a meaningful way and then make the powerful decision to unleash your true potential and live by the rules you set; the rules of your soul, instead of what people think or what the society wants you to live by.

Everything you need is in you. I love this statement that says you don't know how strong you are until *being strong is the only thing to do.* This is so true. Until you push yourself, you don't know what you are capable of.

I'll cite an example of when I started doing planks. Yes, planks. This might seem very little, but I celebrate all achievements, and this is one of them.

The first day, I planked, I could only do it for 30 seconds. Gradually, I began to push myself to see how far I could go or what limit I could get to, eventually, as I began to do this, I realised I could do 45 seconds, it moved to 60, then 90, then 120 and now, I'm sure if I get down to it, I can hold on for 3 or 4 minutes. My point is, if I hadn't pushed myself, I wouldn't have known that it is possible for me to achieve this.

Another example is the one of always thinking that if you had a quantifiable amount of money, you can start one business or another, or achieve certain milestones.

Fair enough, money is needed to achieve certain things, but then again, if you dig deeper, you will find that there are some things you can get done that do not require money to be done. And even if money is required, start with what you have. Break your money into bite sizes and then work on getting the funds in smaller amounts at a time.

When I started the prestigious ELOYs in 2009, we had no money to organize our first event. In fact, 8 years down the line, we still organise the ELOYs successfully, with or without physical cash.

Over the years, I have realised that there are different forms of currencies, and the most important one which people leave out and often forget is the *human relationship* currency.

Over the years, I have formed alliances with people and organisations, and as a result, we now exchange services instead of paying with actual money; it's called contra deals and we have been able to successfully organise our events and run *Exquisite Magazine* based on these relationships.

Like I said earlier, money is needed to achieve certain things, so it cannot be totally ruled out. On the flip side, you cannot base your starting a business on the lack of money. Use your inner power, and use your abilities to find a way to do things creatively.

AFFIRMATIONS:
- I MAKE MONEY EASILY AND EFFORTLESSLY
- I AM HONOURING, LOVING AND EMBRACING MYSELF IN EVERY THOUGHT, WORD AND ACTION.

— *#14* —

FOCUS IS KEY
- YOU CANNOT GET TO YOUR GOAL BY FOCUSING ON THE WRONG THINGS!

Make it a point to hold your focus, and stand your ground. Win in your head first. Don't be bullied by your mind, you have to constantly train your mind to focus on your focus, all the time.

You need to focus on that goal you want to meet, and take every inspired action you require to achieve your goal.

Do not be distracted by fear or doubt or anything that has nothing to do with your vision. Stop muddling things up in your head by focusing on too many things at the same time.

Stop confusing yourself by over-thinking and having negative feelings that have no business with your goal.

I know there will be distractions, but choose your battles wisely. Be wise to know that they are distractions; do not lose sight of what's important.

Stop procrastinating. You don't have to see the whole staircase; you don't have to see the whole plan God has for you – just hold your focus and take the action required.

Take it one day at a time, one goal at a time, cross one hurdle then move to the next. Fight for your vision.

Focus is key.

Remember the bible says ask, believe and receive.

For you to be in the *receiving and believing stage,* you need to focus on what you want with a positive attitude and energy, knowing everything would turn out right.

With the right attitude, the right ideas will start to come to you – I call them inspired action steps that are required for you to achieve your goal.

This is what I do: I write out my goals and I stare at them as many times in a day as possible. When I get ideas from my subconscious, like my inner mind is speaking to me, I act on those actions, because those ideas are the guiding light I require to achieve my targets.

We only have one life to live; we might as well make it grand by living it intentionally!

I take it one day at a time, one goal at a time.

If your plan is to own your own home by a certain time, yes you need to work towards it – but what are you doing with what you have currently? When you get an inflow of funds, are you putting some aside for this new home you desire? Are you caring for the one you currently live in? Are you taking action steps in faith to acquire this property? Steps such as looking for this new home, and when you do find the home you desire, going ahead to speak to a mortgage company.

If you currently live in a rented property, are you grateful for it, nurturing it and living in it like it's your own? You need to focus on what you have now, embody home ownership and see how things will shift in your favour when you own your own home.

Don't be distracted by the fact that you live in a rented property, don't be distracted by thoughts of *I shouldn't be here,* or just stressing over thoughts you have no business with.

Focus on your *focus,* and do what is required. Don't sabotage yourself with negative thoughts.

AFFIRMATIONS:
- I AM TOO FAITHFUL TO FEAR.
- I WILL FAITH EVERYTHING AND RISE

Mathew 7:7

Tewa's Favourite Qoutes

"What things so ever ye desire, when ye pray, believe that ye have received them and ye shall have them."

- Mark 11:24 -

— *#15* —

FEAR IS A SUCCESS KILLER. DON'T GIVE IN TO FEAR – IN FACT, DO IT SCARED.

FACE YOUR FEAR, STARVE IT AND FEED YOUR FAITH WITH ALL THE ATTENTION, POSITIVE THOUGHTS AND ACTION.

THINK – WHAT IF I SUCCEED, INSTEAD OF WHAT IF I FAIL?

Fear not, for I have redeemed you. Isaiah 43: 1

Fear-induced excuses have killed more dreams than anything else.

Inner thoughts such as – *this is the reason why my dream might fail... Will people like this idea? Why are you even doing this or that?* – are led by fear.

The battlefield is in the mind, and within your head space; your inner voices are constantly at war and you possess the power to choose which path is true for you.

Only you can decide which is true for you. Only you.

Note that whenever you take action, you are overcoming your fears. Don't be bullied by your mind; get into the habit of taking action, and always doing something, regardless of what the situation is.

Don't give any time to your fear; fill your time with action. Get busy doing something; you can pray, even while you're making your bed, clearing your desk, running, cooking – just do something... *anything*, to starve the doubt and fear.

Do not sit down pondering, thinking of the challenge, waiting around and wishing for things to change; all these actions are actually feeding the fears and doubt. You need to feed your faith.

Don't let doubt and fear control you anymore from becoming the person you want to be. Fill your time with purposeful events; this is what I call *living intentionally*.

Living intentionally is deliberately feeding your time with actions that will move you closer to fulfilling your goal.

You can overcome your fear by just moving out of your comfort zone and doing something, you can succeed by simply taking action!

Don't let life happen to you! Living a purpose-filled life starts with you having the mentality of not letting your mind rule you. Rule your mind, instead!
Don't let your mind wander off on its own tangent – take hold of it, and steer it in the direction you want it to go.

I remember an incidence where I accidentally transferred a large sum of money to someone in the middle of the night. I found myself screaming, '*no... no...*' at my phone until I received the message – *transaction successful*. Oh gosh, I wanted to pass out.

Guess what? I had only met the guy who I accidentally transferred the money to once, and I had decided to do business with him because he appeared like someone I could trust. I didn't really know him.

Now, I had to put that trust to test. I called him at about 1am, the time the error had happened. Luckily, he was awake and he promised to send the money back to me as soon as he received it.

My mind started playing games on me – I started thinking, *what if he doesn't send the money back? What if he turns his phone off and runs off with my money?*

I realised almost immediately I started having negative *what if* thoughts, that if I didn't change the way I was thinking, every single thing I was afraid of will come to reality by the following morning. I knew I couldn't just go to sleep because my mind would work on these thoughts and I would unconsciously focus on them till it became my reality.

I had to take hold of my mind, so instead of going to sleep, I started praying and speaking to myself, as loudly as I could in the middle of the night, that he would return my money because it didn't belong to him, and I had worked for it. I did this till I had successfully convinced myself that he would send it back.

At about 3am, I got an alert. He had sent a portion of the money. He called me to say that the money he had sent was his bank account's online transfer limit, and he would go to the ATM first thing in the morning to transfer the rest.

Can you believe my mind still wanted to bully me into having negative thoughts by thinking: *Yes, so what? He transferred some of the money – he will surely abscond with the rest!*

I had to arrest my thoughts again till I was sure no negative thoughts were filtering through my mind. I went on and on with this battle, but in the end, by 11am the following day, he transferred all the money to me.

This is an easy example, but the bottom line is: you have to be deliberate and take hold of your mind.

Being deliberate and taking control of your mind can be applied to everything in your life; from wanting to eat a certain type of meal to wanting to marry a particular partner. Just focus and believe and say it to yourself like you mean it.

You should be too busy taking action – positive action – so it should be easy to feed your faith.

Take an action – even if it's a little step; just keep it moving, don't be idle for too long, so it doesn't fully sip into your subconscious. Take hold of your mind, you've got the power to!

AFFIRMATIONS:
- I TRUST MY JOURNEY
- I AM OPEN TO RECEIVING UNEXPECTED BLESSINGS IN MY LIFE

— *#16* —

YOU ONLY SEE WHAT YOUR MIND IS ABLE TO COMPREHEND.

STOP BELIEVING EVERYTHING YOU SEE THAT IS CONTARY TO WHAT YOU DESIRE, BUT BELIEVE EVERYTHING YOU WANT IS COMING TO YOU!

The mind believes whatever you tell it to.

Therefore, it is extremely important to train your mind to only see the positive in everything, and tame your mind to keep it from running wild with negative thoughts and imaginations that are not in line with what you desire.

Win in your head first, and then you will begin to see positive results in your reality. It takes time, and lots of practice.

Practice, practice, practice! This is so important – it's like air to your life, because if you don't practice taming your mind, it will definitely run off on its own tangent.

You can only see what your mind is able to comprehend. If you only see struggles and challenges, you will continue to experience more of that.

You need to stop believing everything that is happening to you. You need to train your mind to see the lessons in whatever challenge you are faced with. Learn the lessons; let them count for something, let them draw you closer to your goal or vision.

Good things come to those who believe they deserve to have them. So expect good things; believe they are coming, and they will come to you whilst you are taking the action required to achieve them.

What are your standards? *Do* you settle for less and simply make do? Do you believe in yourself enough to work on your dream? Are you that passionate about your dream? Or are you just looking for the quick easy route?

Watch what you think and what you base your beliefs on.

Life is as good as your beliefs. If you believe in the worst case scenario, you will always get things in the worst case scenario. If you believe you deserve the best, then you will work at being the best, you will always find yourself doing what is required, not what's easy. You will believe in the best case scenario only.

AFFIRMATIONS:
- I AM READY TO RECEIVE ALL THAT I HAVE PRAYED FOR
- I HAVE THE ABILITY AND RESOURCES TO ACHIEVE ALL MY GOALS

Tewa's Favourite Qoutes

"The secret of achievement is to hold a picture of a successful outcome in your mind."

- Henry David Thoreau -

— *#17* —

**WE HAVE THE POWER TO SHIFT OUR REALITY TO WHAT WE WANT BECAUSE WE HAVE THE ABILITY TO CHOOSE HOW WE LOOK AT THINGS.
CHOOSE RIGHT, LIVE INTENTIONALLY!**

WE HAVE THE POWER TO SHIFT OUR REALITY TO WHAT WE WANT BECAUSE WE HAVE THE ABILITY TO CHOOSE HOW WE LOOK AT THINGS.

One day, I was casually working on my Microsoft Surface device. The battery ran down and I decided to connect it to power and charge it. I was tired from working anyway, and so I decided to go to bed.

The following day, I tried to put the device on, and it refused to come on. I asked a technician to have a look at it, and at the time when it was being looked at, I decided not to be distracted by the fact that my work system was malfunctioning and the fact that I could have potentially lost all my data, as it had been a while since I had done a system back-up.

One of the *Exquisite Magazine* regular events for cervical cancer prevention was approaching, so I decided to focus on that instead. There were certain documents I required for the preparation of this event, and I had an intuition to not think about my faulty Microsoft Surface, but to search our email server for any document I needed to use.

Each time I needed a document, I would do a search on the email server, and believe me, I would find that document. All the proposals I needed and everything was available to me without having to search my work station, which still was not working.

A few days later, I was given the bad news – my Surface device was never coming on again. Something had gone wrong – and then a series of technical jargon.

At this time, our event was just a week away, and I couldn't afford any distractions of the sort.

I went on as normal, even though I was sad for a minute that I couldn't use my Surface. I did think of all my files, but I decided not to dwell on the negative fact of the situation. Instead, I focused on the fact that I was blessed to find most of the documents I needed on the server, and I carried on.
A few weeks later, a friend of mine gave me a laptop, and my work continued as normal.

If I had focused on all the negativity of that situation, more things to feel bad about would have arrived. I probably would never have thought about doing a search on the server, because I would have been too focused on the loss of my data. I would not have been able to successfully plan our event, because I would have been distracted by the fact that I had no system to work with, and to crown things, I had lost all my data.

This little illustration goes to show that we have the ability to change the outcome of any situation; it just depends on how we look at it, and how we react to it.

Don't be bullied by your mind, you have the power, choose right!

AFFIRMATIONS:
- I AM GRATEFUL FOR ALL THE GOOD THAT HAS COME INTO MY LIFE AND ALL THAT IS YET TO COME.
- I AM CREATIVE AND DIVINELY GUIDED IN ALL I DO

— *#18* —

YOU ARE GOOD ENOUGH.
YOU ARE WORTHY.
AND YOU ARE ENOUGH!

I'll tell you a very short story about something that happened when I was in
England. Several years ago, I decided to start a magazine for women of colour. At the time, there were not many magazines available for women of colour in England, and of the few that existed, none were sold in Tilbury, Essex, where I lived. I thought to myself that instead of complaining, I might as well start one!

The only qualification I had was my degree in the Pharmacology , my transferable skills from University, experience I had gained from working in different Pharmaceutical companies, my talent for writing, my love for fashion and my ever supportive family.

Fair enough, maybe I was lucky to have those, but my point is, at that moment, I was inspired and I motivated myself, because I somehow knew and believed I was enough.

I didn't know the first thing about publishing, but I knew I could learn. I found people who helped strengthen my weak points and I was willing to learn. I believed that with my God given talent of writing and my love for fashion and more, I could do it.

Yes, when you take this approach, mistakes will be made, and lessons will constantly be learned, but you have to resolve within yourself, and win that battle within yourself, and tell yourself that you are enough and you are worthy.

With that belief, you begin to realise your strengths and weaknesses, and then you get knowledge and associate with people who will help overlap in areas of your weaknesses.

It's not going to be easy, because you have to step outside your comfort zone, but it starts with you – with you believing in yourself, creating and writing down a plan and then following up with action steps.

ACTION is required. You can't sit there thinking and knowing you are enough with no action. You also have to move out of your comfort zone. You can't read and listen to all the motivational stuff, and not put pen to paper and act.

You have to act, and just like committing to brushing your teeth twice a day, you need to keep getting motivated and inspired by your goals and plans, and ensure that the fire keeps burning.
Start with this notion that you are good enough, you are worthy and you are enough!

You are God's highest form of creation and you have been born to win!

AFFIRMATIONS:
- I ONLY EXPECT THE BEST-CASE SCENARIO
- I NEVER GIVE UP

Tewa's Favourite Qoutes

"Don't wait until everything is just right. It will never be perfect. There will always be challenges, obstacles and less than perfect conditions. So what? Get started now! With each step you take, you will grow stronger and stronger, more and more skilled, more and more self-confident, and more and more successful."

- Mark Victor Hansen -

— *#19* —

GRATITUDE, VISUALISATION, FAITH, AND THE FEELING OF HAVING IT ALREADY, ARE REQUIRED TO TURN THINGS AROUND FOR YOUR GOOD.

GRATITUDE, VISUALISATION, FAITH, AND THE FEELING OF HAVING IT ALREADY, ARE REQUIRED TO TURN THINGS AROUND FOR YOUR GOOD.

> *In everything give thanks, for this is the will of*
> *God in Christ Jesus concerning you.*
> *1 Thessalonians 5:18*

> *Do not be anxious about anything but in everything*
> *by prayer and petition, with thanksgiving, present your request to God.*
> *Philippians 4:6*

Be too thankful to worry – God's got this! He is turning everything around for your good.

Visualisation is important. Faith Everything And Rise – this is my definition of FEAR.

> *Set your mind on the things above, not on earthly things.*
> *Colossians 3:2*

See your goals as already achieved. If you can't see it in your head, you can't hold it in your hand. Work and act like the only possible outcome is success.

See it in your head and mind, say it with your mouth, and get it by taking actions that propel you towards your desire.

GRATITUDE, VISUALISATION, FAITH, AND THE FEELING OF HAVING IT ALREADY, ARE REQUIRED TO TURN THINGS AROUND FOR YOUR GOOD.

Be filled with praise, be joyful, and be grateful for God's mercy and grace. *He* will see you through; just ensure you are doing something that He can bless. Take Action! Have faith! Believe! It's in your hands.

One thing I have come to realise is that you cannot fake happiness. Well, you might pull it off when you're in front of a crowd of people, but when you are alone, by yourself, you cannot fake being *truly* happy.

For you to be happy enough to manifest happiness as an emotion, you need to show some gratitude.

This is tried and tested, and you can try it too. If you want to become intentionally happy, just start thinking of all the things you are grateful for. Believe me, within a few seconds, a smile will start to curl on your face, and you will unknowingly start feeling joy and happiness.

For me, gratitude is the quickest way to feel happiness. Since being happy is my main goal, I am always intentionally looking for things to make me feel gratitude, and in turn feel happiness.

I have realised that the more I focus on being grateful and showing gratitude, the more I get into situations that bring me more things to be happy about.

Try it, it works!

AFFIRMATIONS:
- WINNING IS MY BIRTHRIGHT
- I AM PAYING ATTENTION TO THE RESULTS I WANT

— *#20* —

STOP LIVING OUT YOUR FEARS;
CHOOSE TO LIVE OUT YOUR DREAMS BY CHANGING YOUR THINKING, AND ACTING LIKE THE WINNER YOU ARE MEANT TO BE.

The current state of your life is as a result of your past thoughts, which have led you to taking certain actions and reactions that have made your life turn out as it is today.

Daily, we are living our fears, because we have been programmed to think of the worst case scenario first, and then adapt to it.

I decided to take hold of my mind and be aware of my thoughts by determining which thoughts were limiting me, and which ones were uplifting me. I learned to do this by feeding my spirit with enthusiasm and positivity, and I practiced this daily.

You have to fight for that self awareness because your subconscious mind will believe only what *you* tell it.

My dream is for you to master yourself to the point where it becomes second nature to be filled with so much positive energy, fear starves to death.

Are you serious about your dream life? Then take hold of your mind.

Change your thinking; act like the only result possible is success; dress for success, and show up like God's highest form of creation (There is a difference between confidence and arrogance though, watch out), and go and make it happen!

Making this happen is work in progress too; results won't happen overnight. It needs constant practice, being consistent and the determination to rise.

A great indicator is if you realise that the life you're currently living is not what you desire, this means you are thinking more of what you don't want, and less of what you do want.

Switch your thoughts! Think and focus on what you do want, and watch your life experience change accordingly because, whatever you focus on, grows. Remember that.

Don't let your mind bully you, train it well; practice makes perfect, you *can* rule your mind.

AFFIRMATIONS:
- I WILL SUCCEED AT WHATEVER I SET MY MIND TO DO
- I CAN DO VERY WELL AT ANYTHING I SET MY MIND TO DO

Tewa's Favourite Qoutes

"Whether your thoughts and feelings are good or bad, they return as automatically and as precise as an echo."

- Rhonda Byrne -

— CHAPTER 21 —

YOU ARE WHERE YOU ARE NOW AS A RESULT OF YOUR THOUGHTS AND THE WORDS YOU SPEAK.

CHANGE YOUR FUTURE INTENTIONALLY, BY CHANGING YOUR THOUGHTS AND SPEAKING ONLY OF WHAT YOU WANT.

Control your thoughts, as it helps control how you feel. You need to think positive and happy thoughts; speak only of what you want to manifest and become your reality.

You will be able to change your thoughts to happy ones, by being present in the *now*. Realise how blessed you are and be thankful for that.

Once you begin to say *thank you* for your blessings, your mood will definitely begin to change and you will attract more things to be grateful for.

If you can visualise it, feel like you have it already. In a short period with those happy thoughts, feelings and spoken words, you will receive it. You don't need to say it to people. Say it to yourself all the time.

Control your thoughts, be aware of them. An example is this: if you think to yourself "I'm going to have a great day" and feel that, you will have a great day. Same applies if you say otherwise. To receive your desire, you have to *feel it* into being. You are going to feel something anyway – you might as well choose happiness.

I have found that the fastest way to feel happiness to be filled with gratitude. Be grateful for what you have in your life now, and be thankful for it. As you begin to count your blessings, your mood will begin to lift and you will begin to realise that you are blessed. This feeling will attract more things to be happy about, to you.

Yes this is repetitive, and sounds like Qoute #19. I intentionally made it so, to remind us that we need to be deliberately filled with gratitude, to deliberately feel happiness!

AFFIRMATIONS:
- I CHOOSE TO HAVE UPLIFTING THOUGHTS ONLY
- I CHOOSE TO BE HAPPY

— *#22* —

YOU WILL BECOME UNSTOPPABLE WHEN YOU HOLD ON TO BELIEFS THAT SUPPORT YOU AND LIFT YOUR SPIRIT.

When you believe in yourself, you become unstoppable. If one door doesn't open, don't dwell on it; move on to the next door – just keep it moving.

When you hold on to beliefs that support you, you will feel better about your present reality, and look forward to the great future you want. It's not all in a day's job, but you can achieve this with constant action and practice.

Supporting beliefs include loving yourself and being filled with gratitude, as opposed to worry; and thinking highly of yourself, not down on yourself. What you believe about yourself matters a great deal.

I say to people that your mind is your biggest enemy, if not utilised properly. We have the power to think and *feel things* into being. The more worrying we focus on, the more things to worry about we get, so why worry? Channel that energy instead into being happy in the present.

Today is just a part of the journey, a part of the story. Enjoy the process with gratitude and great faith.

AFFIRMATIONS:
- I AM HAPPY
- I AM RICH

Tewa's Favourite Qoutes

"Nurture your mind with great thoughts, you will never go any higher than you think."

– Benjamin Disraeli –

— *#23* —

BELIEVING IS SEEING. YOUR MIND IS A CREATIVE POWER HOUSE. YOU CAN'T SEE WHAT YOU WANT AS YOUR REALITY IF YOU DON'T BELIEVE IT. USE YOUR MIND RIGHT.

*And if we know that he hears us – whatever we ask – we know that we
have what we have asked him*
1 John 5:15

If you know the power you have with your mind, you will never have a negative thought again.

If you realise how creative your mind is, you will only feed it with content that uplifts you.

My sisters and my kids (my hubby has now gotten used to it) always think it's amusing that I don't watch horror movies, or that I restrict myself from reading, listening or watching certain media that I have termed *inappropriate*. I tell them that my imagination is unbelievable. I have come to know myself.

When I was much younger, anytime I watched a horror movie or listened to sad stories, I would recreate those thoughts in my head to the point that they became so real that I believed them, and they frightened me.

When I realised this, I stopped watching or doing anything that I knew would recreate negativity in my head. Unknown to me then, I was practicing mastering and knowing myself. I was fine-tuning the art of self awareness.

Believing is definitely seeing. If you don't believe it, it cannot be seen. I have tried this so many times to know that we have been programmed to think *seeing is believing*, but, in living the life you desire, you have to believe it's possible first, before it manifests and becomes your reality.

The phrase: *seeing is believing*, means seeing it in your mind first (visualisation), then believing it will happen, then, you see it in your reality (receiving).

I'm still learning, and with every mountain I climb, a new level of awareness is required. I fight the good fight of faith, and I keep increasing my awareness and belief ante.

The battlefield is in the mind, the place where you constantly have a conversation with yourself. What you believe is true, is what occurs in your reality.

Nothing comes into existence by focusing on what you can see on the outside, which is probably not what you want. Everything comes from the thoughts and feelings you experience *within;* everything comes from believing on the inside first that *it is possible!*

What version of you do you see in your mind? Who do you see yourself as in your mind or who do you believe you are in your mind?

You were born to win!

AFFIRMATIONS:
- MONEY IS MY FRIEND
- I WILL ARISE AND SHINE FOR MY LIGHT HAS COME

— *#24* —

THE SECRET TO HAVING IT ALL IS BELIEVING YOU ALREADY DO, BY ACTING AND SPEAKING LIKE THE TRUE WINNER YOU ARE!

The Secret To Having It All Is Believing You Already Do, By Acting And Speaking Like The True Winner You Are!

Act like the only possible outcome is success.

Focus on the best-case scenario only.

Work like you already know you will win.

Get out of your comfort zone.

Declare that you have everything you desire with faith. Own it. Starve your fears, and refuse to be bullied by your mind.

In September 2017, during the EMAC Walk/*Smearathon,* a free, all-day cervical-cancer screening marathon event we hold regularly to raise awareness for cervical cancer prevention, it began to rain.

We had been planning this event for months, and on the D-day when we had just arrived at the Muri Okunola Park in Victoria Island Lagos, where the event was to take place, the rain began.

It had started with a light drizzle and before we knew it, it began to pour heavily. There was no way we could have had our walk in the rain. No one dared walk in a downpour of that magnitude, and otherwise risked having a severe flu.

The downpour continued for an hour or more. We had to make an executive decision on what the next action would be, but I knew cancelling the event was never going to be an option.

I had already asked God to *hold the rain* for us that morning, so we could have a great walk and a fantastic *awareness* event. When the rain began, I became aware almost immediately, and I activated my focus mind game. Like I said, cancelling was not an option.

Everyone spoke about the rain except me. I kept saying to anyone who asked me if we were still going ahead, with a bright happy voice, *yes, we will and the rain will stop.*

I said it's not raining so many times to myself till I actually believed it, and I carried on as normal. People must have thought I was crazy and were probably thinking: *"yeah, right!"*

Lo and behold, just as we were about to start the pre-walk activities, the rain stopped. In fact, it became so sunny, no one would believe it had rained heavily earlier.

My point is, I knew I was going to win that day, come rain or sun; and I didn't let anything happening around me distract me from that focus. I had to take hold of my mind by force and make myself believe I wasn't seeing rain, and from my mouth to God's ears, it worked.

Everything we want in life is available to us; we just have to believe we already have it, and act like the only possible outcome is success.

AFFIRMATIONS:
- I ACT WITH 'GODFIDENCE' AND GRACE
- I AM BOLD

Tewa's Favourite Qoutes

"Your dreams don't have an expiration date. Take a deep breath and try again."

- Udo Okonjo -

— *#25* —

STOP LOOKING BACK. THE FUTURE IS BRIGHT AND IT IS RIGHT IN FRONT OF YOU!

The mind (or the devil) has a way of reminding you about your past, to destabilise you and bring you down. Remember Lot's wife in the Bible? She looked back and turned into a pillar of salt. In other words, if you constantly look back, you will remain stagnant.

Don't let your mind bully you. Stay in control. Be alert and intentionally check the conversations you have with yourself. Have self talks that uplift you, not limit you. Have self talks about what you want, not what you don't want.

Be thankful to God for the past. Be thankful for all things, but remember that the past is the past for a reason; look to the future with high hopes and be filled with gratitude for the lessons learned. Remember those lessons came with tests which you passed, otherwise you wouldn't be where you are today.

Remember, we are all work in progress; for you to get to your next level, you must fully grow from the lessons of your current challenges.

Consistency is definitely key to achieving anything; just keep making yourself better every day, the results of your hard work will come.

AFFIRMATIONS:
- I ACCEPT THE ABUNDANCE THAT IS FLOWING INTO MY LIFE RIGHT NOW
- I AM AT PEACE

— #26 —

WHEN YOU FOCUS ON SOMETHING WITH POSITIVE ENERGY, YOU ARE CALLING IT INTO EXISTENCE.

FOCUS RIGHT, DON'T BE DISTRACTED BY FEAR!

Don't be distracted by things that have absolutely nothing to do with your vision. I know there will definitely be distractions, but choose your battles wisely. Be wise to know that they are just distractions and don't lose sight of what's important.

Remember to ask, believe and receive. For you to receive what you have asked for, you need to believe you deserve it. Focus on what you want with a positive attitude and energy, knowing it will be all right.

Hold that focus, not with worry or fear, and receive your heart's desires; hold your focus with gladness, passion and excitement, knowing and believing that what you seek is also seeking you.

Focus on your focus!

AFFIRMATIONS:
- I AM MORE THAN ENOUGH
- THINGS ARE ALWAYS WORKING OUT FOR ME

Tewa's Favourite Qoutes

"Success is a state of mind. If you want success, start thinking of yourself as a success."

— Dr Joyce Brothers —

— #27 —

LOOK IN THE MIRROR, THAT'S YOUR COMPETITION.

NOW CHANGE WHAT YOU DON'T LIKE, AMPLIFY WHAT YOU DO LIKE AND ACT THE WAY YOU WANT TO BE!

Focus on your *Focus;* focus on what you want. Exercise your mind daily to only think and say positive things, till it becomes second nature.

Act like the only result possible is success. Yes it's repetitive, I have said this before, but we need reminders, I remind myself of this daily.

Stop focusing on your weaknesses or what you don't like, you already have people doing that for you. It'll only make you weaker and more negative. Stop focusing on what people believe about you. Focus on being a better *you*.

Focus on your strengths, amplify them; focus on what makes you happy and get to work.

Roll tape, Action! Act the way you want to be. Dress the way you desire.

I think of myself as a queen, so I carry myself like one. A few years ago, when my son was nine years old, he asked me why I was wearing a particular outfit to a meeting with a potential partner, I replied by saying, *I want them to know I am a queen and should be treated like one!*

He asked me with large believable eyes, "*Mum, are you a real queen?*"

And I said, "Yes, *and you are a king. I am the queen of my world and you are the king of your world, and you can rule it however you see fit.*"

Need I say, the meeting went exceptionally well, and I got what I wanted. I wasn't arrogant about knowing who I am, I just reinforced who I am by how I dressed and how I addressed everyone, with confidence and respect for each individual.

Note there is a difference between being confident and being arrogant. Confidence comes from a place of faith and belief in yourself, while arrogance comes from a place of fear and insecurity.

AFFIRMATIONS:
- ABUNDANCE FLOWS INTO MY LIFE IN SURPRISING AND EXCITING WAYS
- MY DREAMS ARE VALID

— *#28* —

DEVELOP YOUR WILL POWER.
BUILD AN IMAGE IN YOUR MIND AND THEN PUT ALL YOUR FOCUS ON THAT IMAGE!

You need to develop your will power constantly.

You need to make it a point to deliberately develop your will power; the will power to hold an image of what you want in your mind and the will power to not be distracted.

WILL POWER!

Your will power will give you the ability to hold one idea in your mind, and subtract all other distractions.

You need to learn to hold on to the vision in your mind, no matter what; focus on your desired outcome to bring it into reality without thinking of capitalising on any distraction.

When you are trying to focus, all sorts of ideas and scenarios will start popping into your head; but your will power and the determination to win the battle in your head, will help you hold on to thoughts that will keep you focused on your focus.

This takes practice. To activate a strong will power, you have to be willing and ready to elevate yourself, and not remain in the place you do not want to be.

You can start developing your will power by focusing first on things you might consider insignificant, and don't really matter.

For example, a few years ago, to test the strength of my *will-power*, I would focus on getting the car parking space I wanted at any mall or event I attended and believe me, after practicing *focused thinking* a few times, I always got the parking space I desired!

Even at events that were packed to the brim, the security guards always managed to find me a nice spot to park my vehicle without struggle.

Go on, train your mind, and live the life you desire by building it yourself.

Live intentionally!

AFFIRMATIONS:
- I AM RESPONSIBLE FOR MY OWN HAPPINESS
- I CREATE SUCCESSFUL HABITS DAILY

Tewa's Favourite Qoutes

"It is impossible to bring more into your life if you are feeling ungrateful about what you have."

- Rhonda Byrne -

— *#29* —

**MAKE YOURSELF A PRIORITY.
LOVE YOURSELF; IF YOU DON'T, NO ONE WILL!**

Make Yourself A Priority.

It's all part of living the life you desire – you can't love the life you want if you don't love or value yourself.

This means that if you don't make yourself a priority, you will be subject to people's opinions and always do things for other people, and not yourself. You have to take care of yourself first, before you can take care of anyone else.

Do not let your mind bully you into thinking that making other people a priority shows that you love them. Yes, it will show them you care, but at whose disadvantage? Every time you deprive yourself of some form of happiness or joy because you are doing something for someone, you lose that moment to love yourself.

Time-outs are necessary for you to recuperate and get to know yourself even more. If you don't know yourself, how will anyone know how you would love to be loved?

Love yourself enough to fight for your dreams.

Love!

No one can love you like you, so get to it; and do it first for yourself, and other things will follow.

That also goes for your plans and goals. Stop holding yourself back by not loving yourself enough to chase your goals and fulfil your dream.

Tick tock, the time ticks away every second with no care of who is doing what or not.

Love yourself enough to want the best for you, and do what is required.

We are all born to win, let's make it happen!

AFFIRMATIONS:
- I PUT IN THE REQUIRED ACTION TO ATTAIN MY GOAL
- I AM OPTIMISTIC

— *#30* —

WHATEVER YOU ARE THINKING OF NOW WITH FAITH (EXCITEMENT) OR FEAR (WORRY) IS CREATING YOUR FUTURE.

BE AWARE OF YOUR THOUGHTS!

Everything that has happened or will happen to you starts with a thought and the feeling you associate with it. What are you thinking of right now?

The moment you begin to understand that you are creating your future with what you are thinking of *now*, that thought alone will jolt you to think more thoughts in the direction of what you want!

Who wants to worry some more? Who wants to get into more debt? But because we have been programmed to think and worry about our current situation, we forget that thinking and worrying about a challenge only creates more things to worry about.

So be aware. Change your thoughts; if your thoughts are not in line with what you want, do yourself a favour and change them. Do not be bullied by your mind; you own it – you rule it, and rule it to your advantage.

To be in abundance, think wealth, think abundance, think of all the things you will do with the money once you get it; be filled with that joy and happiness, and watch what happens.

Wake up filled with gratitude every day. If you don't *feel like it,* force yourself to feel like it by only thinking of the things you currently have that are making you happy.

Trust me; you will find something to be thankful for and as you do that, more things to be grateful for will start appearing in your reality.

Don't just take my word for it, try it!

AFFIRMATIONS:
- I DO EVERYTHING WITH THE CERTAINTY THAT IT WILL GO MY WAY
- I DESERVE ALL THE GOOD THINGS IN LIFE

Tewa's Favourite Qoutes

"Our words have creative power. Whenever we speak, either good or bad, we give life to what we are saying"

- Joel Osteen -

— CHAPTER 31 —

STOP PROCRASTINATING. IF IT'S IN YOUR HEART TO DO IT, GO FOR IT! DON'T GIVE IN TO FEAR-INDUCED EXCUSES!

Fear-induced excuses have killed more dreams than anything else; don't give into those fears.

Acknowledge and realise that the fear is there, but move past it by filling your mind with positive thoughts of faith in the unseen.

Stop procrastinating; what better time to start on your dream than now? If you don't start now, you will only regret months or years later.

To be great, you have to start first!

Change your mindset and see that procrastinating will only delay the manifestation of your desire; and of what benefit is that to you if you don't get your desire?

Don't let the fear of failure affect your state of happiness today. Why are you even thinking of failing at something that you have not started?

You haven't asked, you haven't made the call, you haven't taken the action, yet you already feel it would fail... Why???

What if they say Yes?

What if they say *No?* At least when you get a *No,* you know to move on to something else...

What if you *fly?* What if that action is what is required for you to *step up?*

Yet we go around already planning the worst-case scenario in our minds. Don't let your mind bully you. Take control!

How about just focusing on the best case scenario and living intentionally by being happy about everything that can go right? How about that? Find things that will make you focus on what you want.
I use reminders, I list things I'm grateful for daily (I call it my winning list or log), I surround myself with things I like, and I use a vision wall, amongst other things.
Procrastination is time wasting. Go for it, even if you think you are not prepared. Learn, as you go along.

I didn't know what I was doing when I started *Exquisite Magazine,* the ELOY Awards and my *Live Intentionally with Tewa* Mastermind, but I started from my basic knowledge anyway and acquired more knowledge as I progressed.

You need to start from where you are and watch as things begin to align in your favour.

You just need to try it to believe it works.

AFFIRMATIONS:
- I AM UNIQUE
- I AM OUTSTANDING

— *#32* —

**FEED YOUR FAITH
BY BELIEVING
EVERYTHING THAT IS
HAPPENING TO YOU IS
FOR YOUR OWN GOOD,
TO GROW YOU!**

When you start seeing the best in all situations, little by little, one step at a time, you will train your thinking to transform your life.

You have to make the decision to only expect great things.

Has being a pessimist worked in any way?

Go into today with happiness and a massive dose of faith.

Live, love, eat well and act like the only result possible is success. Like Jesus, be unbothered about the storm.

Focus. You were born to win!

Don't lower your expectations because of fear or what people will think of you. Make your expectations your exact desire.

Start being optimistic about what can go right; start being positive about what can go right, and be certain.

Plan to be happy now; worrying or pessimism has helped no one. If you plan for the worst-case scenario, you will get the worst-case scenario.

Change your thinking, change your life.

You have to constantly focus on the positive and see the best in all situations. It's a habit that has to be constantly worked on.

Mark 4:37-39

If you are filled with gratitude all the time and always being positive, you attract more of that positivity into your life.

Don't believe the hype, you don't create a better future by being unhappy and depressed; you create a better future by being happy, showing gratitude for your current journey, doing what you should be doing, and enjoying the process because you are creating a better future which God has ordained for you.

So use your faith and stretch it by believing, regardless. We are all born to win.

Today is another great day to make it happen and takeover!

AFFIRMATIONS:
- I EMBRACE MY DIFFERENCE
  I THINK, SPEAK AND WORK ON THE THINGS THAT UPLIFT ME

Tewa's Favourite Qoutes

"Begin to expect great things and you will receive great things. Expect only the best-case scenario"

- Tewa Onasanya -

— *#33* —

DON'T STAY QUIET. IF YOU NEED HELP, ASK FOR IT!

Do not stay quiet. If you need help, ask for it.

That's why we have mentors – people you look up to that can advise you, people who are more experienced and are already doing what you would like to do.

These mentors don't have to be in the same field as you are, but you need to see them as knowledgeable, no matter how old they are.

I'm not saying take their ideas and run with them, but take the lessons – the right ones, you can learn from them, and learn from their mistakes. We don't know it all, but the life maps of other people are there to guide us.

Don't be afraid to ask for help. Learning is done through listening, reading and acquiring more knowledge. If the person you ask is not willing or able to provide answers at any given point, be wise enough to know when to keep it moving and keep trying. Don't take it personally by pestering or thinking ill of that person; they might just not be able to give you what you require at that point in your life or their life.

There is always someone out there that will be a guiding light for you, be on the lookout. This person doesn't need to know you or meet you physically. There are so many people – *far away mentors* – who inspire me and I have never met them, but their messages resonate with me.

Fair enough, I might not be able to communicate with *far away mentors,* but they are living examples of what I would like, so it also works. When I listen to them speak, they answer some of the questions I might be searching for answers to.

Don't be afraid to ask for help and directions in life. You can only do more through learning and acquiring more knowledge.

AFFIRMATIONS:
- I HAVE THE ABILITY TO CREATE
- I AM LIMITLESS

— *#34* —

DON'T WAIT FOR ANYONE TO ENCOURAGE YOU. ALWAYS MOTIVATE AND ENCOURAGE YOURSELF!

Do not wait for anyone to validate you. You might be waiting a long time. Appreciate and encourage yourself.

You are not where you were yesterday. You might not be where you want to be right now, but ensure you are working towards getting there.

Encourage yourself; celebrate and applaud where you currently are, even if you know you can do better. Realise that, and then go and do better.

No one knows your journey better than you do, and Lord knows you have come a long way.

No one knows your vision better than you do, so you have to get a move on. Encourage yourself, motivate yourself to be better, see the great light at the end of that tunnel and be excited you have come this far, and will go beyond.

Today is another great day to work on your dream. Take a minute to appreciate your now, because your tomorrow will be better.

Give yourself a round of applause!

AFFIRMATIONS:
- I WILL LIVE IN THE MOMENT AND BE FILLED WITH JOY AND GREAT EXPECTATIONS
- I AM A POSITIVE ATTRACTION FOR ABUNDANCE AND GREAT HEALTH

Tewa's Favourite Qoutes

*"Whatever ye shall ask in prayer,
believing, ye shall receive."*

- Matthew 21:22 -

— #35 —

**LIFE WILL GO ACCORD-
ING TO HOW YOU ARE
FEELING.
FEEL GOOD TO ATTRACT
MORE GOOD.
THE FEELING YOU GIVE A
SITUATION DETERMINES ITS
OUTCOME!**

Life Will Go According To How You Are Feeling.

How you choose to feel determines if you get a good outcome or otherwise.

Don't let negativity get the best of you.

Always look for the best in everything, no matter how small that best is. Focus on that to lift your spirit.

You need to constantly be on a *feeling good* level to be able to attract more good to yourself.

You are going to *feel* anyway, you might as well feel good. What's the best that can happen?

If you can't attach a good thought and feeling to a particular situation, take your focus away from the bad thoughts and be grateful with the thought that the situation happened to open you up for the better, and that you are learning from it.

Trust the process and trust your journey. *You* decide how to react to things, you decide the outcome; choose which outcome suits your life.

Choose the brighter side!

AFFIRMATIONS:
- I AM HEALTHY
- I BECOME WHAT I TALK ABOUT, I AM A BLESSING.

— *#36* —

THE PRACTICE OF INTENTIONAL AND DELIBERATE THINKING IS ALL THAT STANDS BETWEEN YOU AND EVERYTHING!

THE PRACTICE OF INTENTIONAL AND DELIBERATE THINKING IS ALL THAT STANDS BETWEEN YOU AND EVERYTHING!

Everything requires practice.

It takes practice to walk, run, eat, ride a bike, plank for two minutes or more; you need to practice deliberate thinking like your life depends on it. Be intentional.

I am taking my power back from my unconscious mind, by paying attention to the result I want, being conscious of my thoughts and actions, and nothing else.

I stay focused.

There are too many distractions, and too many things reminding you of the goals, plans, and actions that you have to take. Work at being focused!

There are also the voices in your head that want to keep reminding you why your plans cannot work – be aware! Stay awake! Acknowledge the negative thoughts, and then dismiss them by re-focusing on what you want, and do what's required.

There is no point dwelling on worry lane or feeling inadequate street. Take hold of your mind and grab your will power back!

Fight the good fight for the result you want, after all, you were born to win; it just depends on how much you want to win and how willing you are to put in the work required.

AFFIRMATIONS:
- I AM ABLE
- I AM CAPABLE

Tewa's Favourite Qoutes

"It is important to feel good, to be happy, because when you are feeling good you are putting yourself in the frequency of what you want."

- Marci Shimoff -

— *#37* —

YOU HAVE TO LEARN TO PUSH YOURSELF, SO AS TO BECOME STRONGER AND BETTER.

TAKE SMALL, DECISIVE AND PURPOSEFUL STEPS. STOP STARTING AND STOPPING!

You have to learn to push yourself every minute, every hour, every day. It's a continuous process. Your dreams have to get to a point where they are bigger than your fears, and you must ensure you push yourself to go the extra mile.

You need to push yourself to do the harder, uncomfortable things which are required to make you a better version of yourself.

Today, I dare you to make that phone call you have been procrastinating; I dare you to go the extra mile to fulfil your dream. I dare you to do what you know is required for your next level.

Everything takes time, but you need to start. Start by pushing yourself every single day.

Life is constantly moving with time, and with time you begin to self-push effortlessly, because you know you can do it.

We are all unique and born with the abilities to make our dreams a reality. The difference is in the willingness to get out of your comfort zone to make it happen.

Arise and shine, your time has come; Today is another great day to make it happen!

So As To Become Stronger And Better.

AFFIRMATIONS:
- I AM RECEIVING ALL THE GOOD IN MY LIFE
- I GLOW – HAPPINESS RADIATES FROM ME LIKE SUNSHINE

— *#38* —

YOU HAVE TO BE MENTALLY PREPARED FOR YOUR SUCCESS SO WHEN THE OPPORTUNITIES COME, YOU WILL RECOGNISE AND SEIZE THEM!

You have to be mentally prepared and positively tuned into your success.

Your focus needs to be clear on the results you want, and nothing else. Where you focus your mind, energy will flow, and you will get inspired ideas as you hold that focus.

You prepare your mind by removing all doubt, believing the only result possible is success, and getting to work.

Surround yourself with like-minded people and be alert.

Opportunities come in different ways; be prepared to recognise and tune into them.

We are all born to win!

AFFIRMATIONS:
- I AM LIKE A WELL-WATERED STREAM, EVER FLOURISHING AND EVER-BEARING GREAT FRUITS.
- I AM EXPERIENCING LUXURIANT GROWTH IN EVERY AREA OF MY LIFE

Tewa's Favourite Qoutes

"Take the money in your wallet and invest it in your mind and in return, your mind will fill up your wallet."

– Benjamin Franklin –

— *#39* —

START BEING POSITIVE ABOUT WHAT CAN GO RIGHT!

Since childhood, we have always been told and subconsciously programmed to always think of the worst-case scenario. Who thought to share that belief with the world?

That person or people imposed their limiting beliefs on the whole world.

I reject that. You should too, for your own sake.

Do yourself a favour, change your mindset, and reprogram your subconscious to focus on the *best-case scenario*. It won't be easy, but you have to fight for it.

Who has worry helped? Who has being sad about a situation helped?

Thinking and focusing on the worst-case scenario, just brings it to life, because you have put all your negative energy, thoughts and focus into it. It's like hitting a bull's eye with the darts. You have zeroed in on what you don't want with focused thoughts and energy.

Why not use that energy and focus positively? Fear is the worst case scenario. Faith is the *best-case scenario*. Faith everything and rise!

Faith says to you – ask and it shall be given to you; ask believing you have received. If that is the case, why not just focus on the best-case scenario?

You have to stay positive and believe without a shadow of doubt that things will go right. You have to win that fight in your head. Don't let your mind bully you into thinking otherwise, and don't let your mind give you examples of why the outcome of a situation won't go according to what you desire.

The minute you start focusing on an outcome you do not want, you invite it into your reality.

Fight the good fight with yourself, and win!

AFFIRMATIONS:
- I LIVE IN PROSPERITY AND VICTORY EVERY DAY
- I AM BEAUTIFUL AND WONDERFULLY MADE

— *#40* —

LISTEN VERY ATTENTIVELY TO YOUR IMAGINATION, DREAMS, IDEAS AND FEELINGS; THEY HOLD THE KEY TO YOUR DESTINY (YOUR LIFE PURPOSE)!

What you are searching for almost always comes to you in the form of a dream or another *crazy idea!*

Everyone is destined for greatness, you just have to find that thing that you are passionate about – that thing you love doing – it holds the key to your life's purpose.

People who are living their dreams are people who have mastered their minds to a point where they listen to their inner voice, and they use their imagination to build their own amazing lives. Other people look at them like they are magicians, and that's because they have found what they are good at, and they are maximizing it.

Listen to your subconscious mind; it will guide you towards your life purpose. If the thoughts from your subconscious mind set your soul on fire, then that's what you should be doing. If it makes you jump out of bed excitedly every day, then you should be doing something about those dreams and idea. Otherwise, you will feel unfulfilled, no matter what you do, even if you are earning a million dollars a day.

You can spend your whole life searching for your purpose, passion and place in the world and never find it because what you're looking for is not on the outside, it's on the inside; you are already equipped with it, you just need to dig deep into your soul to find it.

It's something you feel within and it exists in your subconscious mind, your imagination and your dreams.

Pay careful attention to your imagination, dreams and ideas because they are trying to tell you something and that *something* is going to help you become everything you ever wanted.

Go and get your dream life, go and live your dream life, no matter how crazy you think it might be; that might just be what you've been waiting for to propel you to become the best version of you.

AFFIRMATIONS:
- I CAN DO ALL THINGS THROUGH CHRIST WHO STRENTHENS ME
- I'VE GOT THIS. I HAVE ALL I NEED TO SUCCEED

BONUS CHAPTER

— *#41* —

GIVE IT TIME, WORK AT IT, DON'T WORRY ABOUT IT – IT'S ALL COMING TOGETHER.

DON'T BE TEMPTED TO DIG UP THE SOIL TO CONFIRM IF THE SEED IS GERMINATING, JUST TRUST THAT IT IS.

Give it time. Work at it, your desired result is on its way to you. Believe that and you are almost there.

When you plant a seed in the soil, you take action by watering it, and caring for it till it starts to germinate.

In the middle of the growth process, you don't dig up the soil up to check if your seed is growing, do you? You just keep caring for the seed, with the assurance that it is growing.

When it finally sprouts, you don't cut off the tender growth because you haven't seen its fruit yet, you keep taking action by nurturing it till it bears fruit.

The same principle applies to your dream.

When you have a vision, plan, imagine the bigger picture and visualise. Believe you can do it, and keep working at it. Believe that you are growing through it all (the challenges, the good, the not so good) and the fruit of your vision will germinate.

Don't keep uprooting your seed with worry, fear or pessimism. Be optimistic and know your reward is on its way.

I dare you to believe in yourself!

We are all born to win; winning just depends on how much you are willing to fight the good fight of faith for it.

See you at the top – Cheers to your success!

FINAL THOUGHTS

Writing this book has in more ways than a million been a blessing to me! It has helped relive my past experiences which have led me to this point in my life's journey.

This book serves as a reminder. It is not to be read once and put aside, it should be with you at all times, so you can refer back to it, highlight points, and practise tasks to live the life you desire intentionally.

A large part of changing your mindset is to replace incorrect knowledge with positive knowledge that will build you up.

I hope this book has helped you shift and style your mind into thinking you can achieve anything you set your mind to intentionally.

I hope this book in many ways will help you consciously style your mind to look good on the inside so you can have a reality that looks just as good as you see it in your mind; just as you style yourself in your clothes to look good, I hope this book has styled your mind.

I have over 1,000 posts on my own quotes on instagram, and over 100 *#IAffirmbyTewa Affirmations*. I can't share all my quotes and affirmations in one book, but they are available on my social media platforms and also as printed quote boards that are available on sale.

Final Thoughts

To purchase these quote boards, and to access free resources that would facilitate your mind-styling process, please visit: www.tewaonasanya.com

Please let me know how this book has been of benefit to you. I would love to hear your stories, and your thoughts. You can contact me by visiting my website: www.tewaonasanya.com

40 WAYS TO STYLING YOUR MIND

- A Workbook -

1

CHOOSE LOVE. START EVERYTHING FROM THE FOUNDATION OF LOVE.

Write down random acts of kindness which you will offer to specific people today.

The random acts of kindness which I will offer to specific people are:

a. _____

b. _____

c. _____

d. _____

The feedback I received after this exercise is as follows:

a. _____

b. _____

c. _____

d. _____

2

SELF TALK. WATCH THE CONVERSATION YOU HAVE WITH YOURSELF.

What nicknames do you call yourself? Are you fond of saying things like silly me, or how ridiculous of me, or I'm such an idiot? Are you aware of what you actually say to yourself?
The objective of this activity is to listen to yourself, and hear what you say about yourself.

1. The top three phrases I refer to myself currently are:
a._____

b._____

c._____

2. The phrases I would rather use to refer to myself are:

a._____

b._____

3

EXAMINE YOUR CURRENT BELIEFS

What do you believe is true for you? List them.
I believe the following statements are true for me:

a._____

b._____

c._____

d._____

e._____

Do these beliefs get you excited or thrilled? If not, then go back and rewrite your current beliefs. Now, embody that by acting like what you believe.

4

AMPLIFY YOUR STRENGTHS

Daily do things that will showcase your strengths, and not your weakness. If you are better at certain tasks than others, do more of what you are good at. Make a list of your strengths, and ways you can amplify these strengths.

My Strengths are:

a._____

b._____

c._____

I can amplify my strengths by doing the following:

a._____

b._____

c._____

5

FIND YOUR VOICE

Don't be afraid to use your voice. Ask for help if you need to. Positively self-talk to yourself, it would help you believe in yourself. List out some of the things you can do to find your voice:

Some of the things I can do to find my voice are:

a._____

b._____

c._____

d._____

e._____

f._____

g._____

h._____

i._____

6

USE AFFIRMATIONS

Write a list of affirmations and say your affirmations out loud, every time you get the chance to. Write them in your notebook, save the words on your phone. You can even purchase some I Affirm by Tewa Affirmation cards, and use them to create your personalised list of affirmations.

My top affirmations are:

1._____

2._____

3._____

4._____

5._____

6._____

7

TAKE INSPIRED ACTION

You must take steps to make your dream a reality. What do you desire? Why do you want the things you desire? And how would you feel when you achieve these desires? List all the ideas of the things you would require to achieve your goals. Take a moment to think over this, then write down the following:

I desire to have the following things:

a._____

b._____

c._____

d._____

e._____

This is how I plan to achieve the things I desire:

a._____

b._____

c._____

d._____

e._____

When I get these things, this is how I will feel:

a._____

b._____

c._____

d._____

e._____

Enjoy the feeling of achieving your goals already. Take the action.

8

EXPECT TO WIN

List your top expectations for the day. What steps come to your mind to take? Identify the habits that will not serve the steps required to take (this could be waking up late, eating too much, watching too much TV, any habit that will not get you to your goal).

My top expectations for today are:

1._____

2._____

3._____

My habits that can hinder me from achieving my set goals are:

1._____

2._____

3._____

The action(s) I will take to change these habits are:

1._____

2._____

3._____

9

FIGHT YOUR THOUGHTS FOR YOUR DESIRE!

What are you currently thinking of? Do these thoughts make you sad? If yes, intentionally redirect your thoughts to things that will make you happy. It doesn't matter what you chose to think of, it can be of someone that brings you joy, or something you love to di.

Use your affirmations, and enjoy your positive thoughts till any bad thought becomes invisible.

I'm currently thinking of:

a)_____

b)_____

c)_____

My Happy Thoughts Are:

a)_____

b)_____

c)_____

10

FOCUS ON ONE THING AT A TIME

What do you wish to manifest intentionally now? Make a list, and stare at each item on your list till you make yourself believe you have it already. Focus on that feeling. List any inspired action that comes to mind at this time.

I wish to manifest the following intentionally:

a._____

b._____

c._____

d._____

e._____

The inspired actions steps I will take are as follows:

a._____

b._____

c._____

d._____

e._____

Take that action. Do this each time for what you want.

11

BE THANKFUL AND FILLED WITH GRATITUDE

Today, start a gratitude jar. Write one thing or more that you are grateful for each day and throw it into this jar.
List the things and people you are thankful for.

The things and people I am thankful for are:

1._____

2._____

3._____

4._____

5._____

6._____

7._____

8._____

9._____

10._____

12

SEE ONLY THE POSITIVE IN ANY SITUATION

Whatever the situation is, train your mind to see the positive in it, even if it's a small one. If you can't find any positive in a situation, start being positive and thankful for life, the air you breathe, the bright blue sky, and anything beautiful you can think of!

This exercise is to get your mind away from focusing on the negative and looking for positive elements to lift your spirit and create more things to be positive about.

The Positive Things I Can See Around Me Are:

a)_____

b)_____

c)_____

d)_____

e)_____

13

INTENTIONALLY SHIFT YOUR FOCUS ONTO WHAT YOU WANT

What do you want? Make a list of these things, intentionally focus on them, and deal with the things that distract you from achieving them.

I desire to have the following things:

a._____

b._____

c._____

d._____

e._____

I am usually distracted by:

a._____

b._____

c._____

My strategy for dealing with my distractions are:

a._____

b._____

c._____

14

USE YOUR IMAGINATION

Visualise, talk and act like your goals are achieved already. Close your eyes, and see yourself already living as you desire.

Imagine every detail in your head. For example, if you want a successful career or business, imagine how it will feel to run that business, or to have that lavish office you envision. What would you do? How would you dress or address others? What do you see?

Imagine and create as many images as possible in your head, and as you do this exercise, smile like it's already achieved! List ideas that you think of during this exercise.

The ideas that come to me during this exercise are:

a._____

b._____

c._____

d._____

e._____

f._____

15

TELL YOURSELF YOU CAN AFFORD ANYTHING AND CAN DO ANYTHING

List five things that intimidate you, and using affirmations, speak positively about these five things. Get into the habit of saying: "I can afford It", "I can do this!" Be positive that you can achieve anything you desire.

Five things that intimidate me are:

a._____

b._____

c._____

d._____

e._____

My positive thoughts about these intimidating areas are:

a._____

b._____

c._____

d._____

e._____

16

ALWAYS EXPECT THE BEST RESULTS

Say to yourself: "I expect great things!" and list your expectations and how you would feel once you have achieved them.

My expectations are:

a._____

b._____

c._____

d._____

e._____

Once I achieve these expectations, I will feel:

a._____

b._____

c._____

d._____

e._____

Imagine those feelings now and say, thank you!

17

HAVE A VISION WALL TO PLACE IMAGES OF ALL YOUR DESIRES

Look for images of the things you want. Put these pictures up on a wall or in a notebook you can see all the time. You can stick them on the vision wall below.

Write the vision, make it plain. Go to your vision wall or book all the time to remind you of where you want to get to.

18

TAKE A STEP, EVEN IF YOU THINK IT'S SILLY!

Work by faith not by sight. Take some time to think this through.

What do you want? What would you need to get what you want?

List out the unique abilities that you have, it doesn't matter how small. Do you have the resources you require? If No, focus on what you want and go for it! If Yes, just go for it!

I Want the Following things:

a._____

b._____

c._____

My Unique Abilities Are:

a._____

b._____

c._____

To Get What I Need, I Require The Following:

a._____

b._____

c.

19

BE POSITIVE ALWAYS

List 20 things you feel positive about now.
20 things I feel positive about are:

1	11
2	12
3	13
4	14
5	15
6	16
7	17
8	18
9	19
10	20

20

BE PERSISTENT, CONSISTENT AND DETERMINED TO WIN

Persistence and determination are omnipotent. Keep taking positive steps in the direction of your dreams and desires, and one day it will yield great results. Giving up should not be an option.

What action steps have you taken towards your plan or goal or vision?

Did you get positive results from these steps? If no, look at your plan again and try again. Remember, failure is a form of feedback to check your plan and modify it.

I have taken the following actions steps towards my plan or goal or vision:

a._____

b._____

c._____

Ways I'm Modifying My Original Plan:

a._____

b._____

c._____

21

IDENTIFY YOUR PASSION

Identify and list the things you are passionate about. How do you feel when you do any of these things that you are passionate about? Identify what makes you happy, and do more of that.

I am passionate about:

a._____

b._____

c._____

d._____

When I follow my passion, I feel:

a._____

b._____

c._____

d._____

22

BELIEVE IN YOURSELF

Believe in yourself, and your super power. Read your affirmations. Always believe in yourself and your abilities no matter what
List ten positive affirmations:

1._____

2._____

3._____

4._____

5._____

6._____

7._____

8._____

9._____

10._____

23

TAKE A MOMENT TO MEDITATE AND COLLECT YOUR THOUGHTS

This is very important. Today, cross examine yourself and consciously watch what you think of today. Think only positive and creative thoughts, and make a note of them.

The positive and creative things I thought about today are:

a._____

b._____

c._____

d._____

e._____

24

ALWAYS THINK OF THE BEST-CASE SCENARIO

What results do you desire? List them. Then think only of the best-case scenario. Think of the positive that would come out of every situation.

I desire the following results:

a._____

b._____

c._____

d._____

e._____

f._____

g._____

h._____

i._____

j._____

25

GIVE YOURSELF A SELF-EXAMINATION

Determine what you want and why you want it. Do this as often as possible. If what you don't want is still your current reality, then check that your thoughts and actions are in alignment with what you desire.

My top affirmations are:

a._____

b._____

c._____

d._____

e._____

26

SPEAK ONLY OF WHAT YOU WANT

Only speak of what you want and nothing else. It's alright if people think you are crazy, always ensure that your words align with what you desire – that's more important.

The things I want are:

a._____

b._____

c._____

d._____

e._____

27

ASK FOR HELP

Don't be too shy to ask for help. List areas you need help with, and identify the people that might be able to help you.

Reach out to these people and don't be defeated if you don't get the help immediately; trust that the people you need will be available for you.

The areas I need help with are:

a._____

b._____

c._____

d._____

e._____

People that might be able to help me are:

a._____

b._____

c._____

d._____

e._____

28

KEEP A WINNING LOG

Create a winning log where you record all the good things that happen to you. Write in it every day, and be thankful for each entry in your log.

Winning Log

	Date	I'm thankful because...
1		
2		
3		
4		
5		
6		
7		

29

BE INTENTIONAL IN ALL YOU DO

Deliberately do tasks that will ultimately get you to your desired goal. What are you doing now? In what ways are they in line with what you want to manifest in your life?

These are the tasks I am doing right now:

a._____

b._____

c._____

d._____

e._____

These are the ways my current tasks are in line with what I want to manifest in my life:

a._____

b._____

c._____

d._____

e._____

30

FEEL GOOD!

Always feel good, no matter what. A quick way to feel good is to be thankful for all the people and things in your life. No matter how small you think it might be, be thankful for it.

Gratitude Log

People and things to be thankful for	I'm thankful because...
1	
2	
3	
4	
5	
6	
7	

31

DREAM BIG – BE AMBITIOUS

What do you want? Big or small, it takes the same energy and faith; our mind just bullies us into thinking the smaller goal is easier. Don't give in, dream big, be ambitious and believe it's possible. Write out what you dream about.

I dream about:

_____

_____

_____

_____

_____

_____

_____

_____

_____

_____

32

FIND YOUR TRIBE OF POSITIVE PEOPLE

Make a list of all your friends. Next to each name, write how each person makes you feel. If any friend makes you feel less than you are, limit your communication with them. You need people who lift your spirit and challenge you to be better, not people who limit you.

People that add value to my life	The reason why they add value
1	
2	
3	
4	
5	
6	
7	

33

MIND WHAT YOU FEED YOUR MIND

Only consume positive news. Be intentional about the books you read, movies you watch and even the kind of conversations you have. Whatever we consume gets into our subconscious.

Write out the positive things you do every day that makes your mind creative.

The positive things I do every day to make my mind creative are:

a._____

b._____

c._____

d._____

e._____

34

ALWAYS WRITE OUT YOUR PLAN AND GOALS

List out your top three goals, and think through the things that are required to achieve these goals. Find affirmations around your goals, and take action!

My top three goals are:

a._____

b._____

c._____

I require the following to achieve these goals

a._____

b._____

c._____

The affirmations around these goals are:

a._____

b._____

c._____

The actions I am ready to take to achieve these goals are:

a._____

b._____

c._____

35

ADOPT A HEALTHY LIFESTYLE

Do a life edit on some unhealthy habits you might have.

Some of the unhealthy habits I have are:

a._____

b._____

c._____

d._____

e._____

Some of the changes I am making to adopt a healthier lifestyle are:

a._____

b._____

c._____

d._____

e._____

36

CREATE A MORNING MINDSET ROUTINE

Make a list of positive action to take every morning before you get out of bed. For example, my morning mind-set routine includes saying a prayer, listening to my affirmations, and planning my day. Modify this as it suits you.

The positive actions I will take every morning before I get out of bed are:

a. _____

b. _____

c. _____

d. _____

e. _____

37

BE SOLUTION ORIENTATED

Identify the issues that are currently bothering you, and identify what the problems are. List possible solutions, and take action!

The following things are currently bothering me:

a._____

b._____

c._____

d._____

e._____

The possible solutions are:

a._____

b._____

c._____

d._____

e._____

38

BE FLEXIBLE

Always try to adjust to new situations.

The difficult situations I am faced with are:

a._____

b._____

c._____

d._____

e._____

I'm taking the following steps to adjust to these situations:

a._____

b._____

c._____

d._____

e._____

39

BE OPTIMISTIC

Always act like the success you want is inevitable. Write out five affirmations of being successful, and write out things you are hoping would work for you.

Don't be lazy, plan strategically and create a success journal to record your progress.

My Five Affirmations of being successful are:

a._____

b._____

c._____

d._____

e._____

I am hoping the following will work for me:

a._____

b._____

c._____

My Success Journal:

40

LIVE INTENTIONALLY!

You are the architect of your amazing life! From today, decide to take intentional action steps, and go ahead and do that!

I will begin to take the following intentional action steps:

a._____

b._____

c._____

d._____

e._____

f._____

g._____

h._____

i._____

j._____

ABOUT THE AUTHOR

"I love to inspire, motivate and empower people to be the best they can be and best version of themselves. With my wealth of experience over the years, I want to share my knowledge to empower other people!"

-Tewa Onasanya

About The Author

Tewa Onasanya, a Publisher and Mindset Stylist, holds a BSc in Pharmacology from the University of Portsmouth, UK and a certificate in Fashion Journalism from the College of Media and Publishing, UK and is the Founder / CEO of Exquisite Magazine Services Ltd, the publishers of Exquisite Magazine a Fashion, Beauty and Lifestyle Magazine for women.

After graduating from University of Portsmouth as one of the top of her year in 2000, she went on to work in different Pharmaceutical industries including SmithKline Beechams (now Glaxo SmithKline), Roche, Organon in the Netherlands, Arzo Nobel in Germany to name a few. After almost ten years in the Pharmaceutical industry as a Clinical Data Manager, working on research data for medicines, she resigned from her clinical role to focus on Exquisite, her fashion, beauty and lifestyle magazine for women of colour, which she started in 2003.

Exquisite Magazine organises the Exquisite Magazine Annual Cancer Walk, an event aimed at increasing the awareness for cervical and breast cancer and free screening for people. In 2009, Exquisite Magazine started an only female annual awards ceremony called the Exquisite Ladies Of the Year (ELOY) Awards, The ELOY Awards is aimed at celebrating women of excellence in different fields, empowering, motivating and inspiring others. The ELOYS hold on the last Sunday in November.

Tewa also publishes daily motivational and inspiration quotes on her instagram page, and this is aimed at jolting people's thinking to be the best version of themselves. These quotes initially were published under the hash-tag: #emotivatewithtewa and now includes the tags: #mindsetshiftwithtewa #IAffirmbyTewa #Mindsetstylist and #liveintentionallywithtewa.

With her wealth of experience of being an entrepreneur and publisher, a mind-set stylist and the transferable skills acquired from her degree in Pharmacology, Tewa has been invited to and still gives presentations at seminars and conferences.

Tewa Onasanya lives to Inspire, Motivate and Empower herself and others. During her spare time, she loves to burn scented candles whilst reading or writing, loves to cook (she makes the best lasagne in the world), watch movies (especially romance or comedy) with a big bowl of popcorn, swims and she loves shoes.

Tewa Onasanya is married and blessed with two children.

AVAILABLE FROM DECEMBER, 2019

Look out for my next book, **LIVE INTENTIONALLY NOW! Steps to Live the Life You Desire Today,** which will highlight steps and real life stories of how to live intentionally to create wealth, have healthy relationships and achieve optimum health!
The book would focus on the following practical and proven steps that will help you:

Live Intentionally to Create Wealth!

- Have a smart vision
- Practise self constraint on your spending and have a budget
- Save and Invest
- To attract money, focus on wealth. It is highly impossible to bring more into your life if you are focused on the lack of it.
- Use your imagination (this is your power) to make believe you already have the money you want and visualise as often as possible how you will spend it.
- Give money to receive money. This is not to say you should squander your money, its just to say that give willingly and happily and more of it is bound to come back to you.
- Be happy for others. When you hear of or see other people receiving huge amounts of money or being accepted for a contract, be genuinely happy for them.
- Feel happy NOW, even if it hasn't happened yet. Trust that it will and find ways to feel happy now. Go to your winning log, list all the blessings in your life. That will lift your spirit.

Live Intentionally to be in Great Health!

- Laughter attracts joy and reduces negative energy. Find ways to be happy. Watch a comedy show or something. Just be happy.
- Focus on good health and nothing else.
- Don't listen to negative reports. Take advice, do what is required but don't let negative reports set hold on you.
- Focus on what you want and not on what you don't want. You can think your way to perfect health, a great body, perfect weight for you and more with consistent thoughts of what you want.

Live Intentionally to have Beautiful Relationships!

- Love and respect yourself first. When you feel bad about yourself, you attract people and circumstances that will make you feel bad.
- Focus and write out a list of what you love about yourself.
- Make a list of what you love to do.
- Then do those things. When you do things you love and feel better about yourself, you will attract people who are comfortable with that version of you.
- To make a relationship work, focus on the good qualities (positive) of that person and not on the things you complain about (negative). When you focus on good qualities, you get to see more good qualities.

Everything we want is an inside job!
The outer world is the effect of our past thoughts.

Don't let your mind bully you into thinking this current life is the best you can get. Stop thinking of the past, stop feeling sad, and stop thinking of things and experiences you don't want.

Set your thoughts on happiness, and radiate happiness and joy into the world.
Do these things deliberately, be conscious at all times, be intentional and you will soon see the life of your imagination become a reality.
To order, please visit: www.tewaonasanya.com

Reviews

Rule Your Mind is book which many will find useful for taking charge of the mind, a powerful but often uncontrolled asset. This book provides very useful self help resources including affirmations, and winning logs all powerful tools for conquering the never ending battlefield of the mind.

In a world, where most are daily giving up, having access to such a positive well written and authentic resource is invaluable. The battle is truly in the mind, but we have control over it. An easy and straight forward book for self mastery, which is the starting point of all success. You will definitely live by design if you apply the life styling principles which Tewa given her fashion publishing background is uniquely qualified to give. Kudos Tewa.

Udo Okonjo
CEO / Vice Chair Fine & Country West Africa / Founder IWOW (Inspired Women of Worth).

Tewa has written a book that harnesses the inner strength and potential latent in every individual, should they choose to reach deep inside themselves and unleash it.
She posits that it is all a matter of mindset, and encourages us all to make words like, "I can" "I must" "I will" a mantra.
This book is a must-read for anyone who wants to position themselves mentally and strategically to do and achieve great things.

Amaka Chika-Mbonu
Counsellor and Author of 'How To Get Your Wife To Swing From The Chandelier In A Red Negligée'

While Tewa's thinking or thought pattern was challenged in 2012 mine was already disrupted due to a contact at an International conference I was speaking at and met a gentleman who would turn out to become my mentor into the world of adventure sport that took me up Uhuru peak- Kilimanjaro one journey that triggers the reticular Activation system (Ras) for short ,turning one's attention to a heightened sense of awareness and draws one to constantly notice much more.

Making it through (mentally) or around the mountains surrounding us is first and foremost an inside job because that is secret space that all unmovable mountains are moved daily that they will eventually become valleys "styling your mind" happens to us once we open our minds intentionally is what this special book brings to your consciousness "mind-styling " gets the mind stretched to a dimension designed to build resilience amidst setbacks for a comeback because win-ability was strewn into our DNA at birth and daily dedication to our dreams is what this styling of the mind does as there is and will never be any dream that is too extreme or mountain in our minds or life too high to Summit .

To your success,

Dr Joshua Awesome ,

International Keynote Speaker, Stress Doctor, human performance coach & PR consultant

www.ingramcontent.com/pod-product-compliance
Lightning Source LLC
Chambersburg PA
CBHW070527090426
42735CB00013B/2887